Slammin' Sam

Other sports books by George Mendoza

HITTING HOT
  with Ivan Lendl
FISHING THE MORNING LONELY
SECRET PLACES OF
  TROUT FISHERMEN

Slammin' Sam

SAM SNEAD

with GEORGE MENDOZA

DONALD I. FINE, INC.
New York

Library of Congress Catalogue Card Number: 86–82381

ISBN: 0-917657-87-X
Manufactured in the United States of America

10 9 8 7 6 5 4 3 2 1

This book is printed on acid free paper. The paper in
this book meets the guidelines for permanence and
durability of the Committee on Production Guidelines
for Book Longevity of the Council on Library
Resources.

For Don Fine, who loved golf enough to want to do this book.

Special thanks to Stanton V. Abrams, President, Senior Tour Players, Inc., Boston, Massachusetts; Bob Goalby, Gleneagles Country Club; Michael Cohn, Michael Cohn Literary Agency; Deborah Wilburn, formerly Vice-President and Assistant Publisher, Donald I. Fine, Inc.; Rick Horgan, Senior Editor, Donald I. Fine, Inc.; and Robert Viagas, Editorial Consultant. And a special nod to Larry Mullins, former project manager of Gleneagles Country Club.

—*Sam Snead and George Mendoza*

A Word from Bob Hope

I'VE WATCHED SAM play for years and had a lot of fun with him. In fact, it was Sam Snead who said a great line about my golf game. He said, "After you watch Bob swing, you're not sure which restroom he uses."

One can only marvel at the length and success of Sam's professional career. I've heard many stories about the incredible number of years Sam has been playing professional golf. While I don't know the exact year he started, I do know that at Sam's first pro tournament he was paid in Confederate money.

Having played with Sam on many occasions and all over the country, I am still in awe of the perfection of his sweet swing. Even when Sam was not leading a particular tournament, people would follow him just to watch what I and the world consider the most graceful, fluid swing in golf.

Probably what I remember most about playing with Sam is not necessarily his great shot-making but his great storytelling. He would tell backwoods stories with such timing that I began to worry his audiences would be bigger than mine, and considering my game I don't have golf to fall back on.

Often when we played we would trade stories all through the match until the last green (and on to the nineteenth hole). Here the stories stopped and we started trading money, except it wasn't really trading. It was more like me simply handing my money over to Sam.

You might get the impression that Sam is a gambling man, but believe me, Sam never gambles. If he makes a bet there's no risk. He wins on the first tee through shrewd negotiation . . . then just waits until the 18th green to collect. And the stories about Sam's frugality are all true. He made Jack Benny look generous. Many years ago I was told that Sam's mother warned him never to break a mirror because it brought seven years of bad luck. He thought she was talking about a dollar bill. But seriously, folks, as an athlete, Sam is without equal in *any* sport. His achievements as a professional golfer are staggering. He has won major golf championships over *six* different decades.

And Sam cares about people almost as much as he cares about his game. He has helped innumerable charities raise money for their causes. It would be impossible to calculate the amount of money Sam has raised for charities over the years. His special concern has always been childrens' hospitals.

In the end I suspect that Sam's lasting mark will not be his fabled swing, not his seemingly unbreakable record number of tournament victories, but the inspiration he has given to so many, and his ability to excel at his chosen profession long after other athletes have packed it in. The Senior Tour was started because of Sam, and his legacy will be a Senior Tour that for generations will give encouragement to young and old alike, demonstrating that the excitement of golf is a lifetime thing . . . free of age discrimination.

Sam's name is synonymous with good sportsmanship, respect for one's competitor and above all a pure love of the game . . . and a pure love of money. It's only natural . . . John D. Rockefeller, Sr., loved money and he had a bad golf swing. It's a shame Sam never played with him, he could have retired very early.

Preface

CREDITED WITH 135 tournament victories by independent record keepers and 165 by his own account, "Slammin' Sam" Snead is the epitome of the true athletic sportsman.

Sam Snead made his reputation the old-fashioned way, struggling up through a series of open tournaments against the best in the field. Sam Snead's autobiography reveals his unique gift for spinning pithy yarns, a skill planted in him when he was growing up on a farm in backwoods Virginia and nourished during an unprecedented six prize-winning decades.

The man behind the powerhouse swing recounts anecdotes that he previously shared only during those sunny afternoons on the fairway with Jackie Gleason, Richard Nixon and many others. Some stories, I hope you'll agree, are hilarious, some tender and personal—all are filled with the champ's tips and wisdom.

Sam Snead is a member of the PGA and World Golf Halls of Fame and was the tour's leading money winner in 1938, 1949 and 1950. Still active and still winning in the second half of the 1980s, Sam Snead is considered

by many to be the greatest ever to play the game of golf.
His friend Bob Goalby called him the "man who hung
the moon."

—George Mendoza

Chapter 1

A Hillbilly Tune
By Grantland Rice

Sing us a hillbilly lyric again,
Part of the mountainous breed,
Sing us a roundelay, born of the fen,
Focused on Samuel Snead—
Sammy, the golfer, who came from the hills,
Socking the cover off far flying pills,
Sammy, the maker and builder of thrills,
Tell us of Samuel Snead.

Sam was a caddie who picked up a swing,
Sam was a hillbilly kid—
Sam took a wallop at par—and his fling
Gave him an opening bid;
After Sam's wallop, the pellet careens,
Sam has the touch of the satiny green,
Sam's grabbing headlines from Braddocks and Deans—
Good luck to Samuel Snead.

IT WAS AWFUL nice of Grant to have written that. I appreciate his wish of luck. I remember a hell of a lot of times that I needed it. But I always tried to make my own luck, you know?

Folks always painted me like something out of "Li'l Abner," but I'm proud of where I was born, and proud of the folks I came from. Not everyone felt the same way, especially when I first climbed down from the hills and started winning tournaments.

You see, the truth is, the days when I started swinging a club, golf was a rich man's sport, kind of like polo almost. There wasn't hardly any money in it, even for the pros. National championships didn't get you more than a few hundred dollars, but most of those fellas didn't play for the dough.

Golf courses were at country clubs and the people who played on them were country club members, if you know what I mean. Golf is a gentleman's sport, the cleanest sport there is. And it wasn't too long before I was welcome just about anywhere I went. But you can bet that at first they didn't much like seeing a skinny hayseed like me, with my funny clothes and my home-made clubs, coming out on the course and showing 'em how it's done.

I've had a hell of a great life. For some of the pros, after a while, it all gets like a job. It is a lot of work, I won't deny that, but I've never found a kick to beat just whopping that old ball onto the green.

I'd rather spend time with sports people than with any other kind of people. I don't care whether they're friends of mine like Fred Corcoran, or somebody I'm playing against like Ben Hogan. They treat you like a man.

Is golf still a gentleman's game? they ask me. We've never had anything about drugs or stuff like that in golf the way they have in football and baseball, and we never have fights like you have in hockey and basketball. I don't even smoke or drink. Never have.

Golf has changed a lot, of course. Today it's a lot of college kids who have all kinds of theories about this and that. They don't hang around together unless they're rooming together to save some dough. We older pros had to travel together, sharing car expenses and the like, long before jet planes.

But one thing will always be true about golf, and anybody who wants to play golf better remember it: a man who plays football or baseball will come up with a big salary whether he makes a touchdown or a home run. But a golfer, if he don't win and he's not subsidized . . . well, he don't take home too many potatoes.

And hey, you can have a hundred and fifty guys playing golf, seventy-two holes with the rain and wind blowing, and by the fifteenth hole there will be ten guys at the top, all within two shots of each other. And there will be maybe four of them tied. It's unbelievable. Golf requires so much body and mind coordination. With football or baseball you're always in motion. Not with golf. The ball just sits there and looks at you. The thing, I think, is the concentration. There's so little between being first and being second.

And I can tell you, because I've been both.

A lot of them pack it in by the time they're forty, but I just turned seventy-four and I still get out there every day I can. I've been all over the world winning tournaments, but my home is the same property my dad's dad lived in, about six miles from The Homestead in Hot Springs, Virginia, where I'm still the pro.

I was born May 27, 1912, three months behind Byron Nelson and three months ahead of Ben Hogan. My hometown was Ashwood, Virginia, a bitty place in the middle of the Back Creek Mountains, a spur of the Alleghenies. In those last years before World War I, Ashwood didn't have more than four hundred people in it, and it still isn't big enough to show up on most maps. It's pretty, though. Woods full of game and streams full of fish. The best thing about it, looking back, is the fact that it was hiking distance from the town of Hot Springs. The springs all up and down that valley are world-famous and lots of folks come there to take a cure. Some of them play golf along the way, and that's why a golf course was built about three miles from my folks' place on the grounds of The Cascades Hotel.

My dad, Harry Snead, worked at taking care of the boilers for another hotel in town owned by the same folks, The Homestead Hotel. I played my first amateur golf on those courses, and came back for years as a pro. You might say I discovered golf on those courses and always held them in the same regard that golfers in Scotland hold St. Andrews. By the way, the 1987 U.S. Amateur championship is scheduled to be played at the Upper Cascades.

My daddy earned just enough to do for my mother, Laura, and us six kids; Lyle, Homer, Welford (we called him by his middle name, Pete), Jess, Jenny and me. He was a strong man but wiry. He could lift things you wouldn't think possible. On the Snead side they were all rawboned people. He told me about his great uncle who was seven and a half feet and weighted 360. The father was shorter, he was six-six; then they began to marry shorter people and they began to come down. My brother Jess came almost to being a giant. He was about

six-three, and he had wrists on him you wouldn't believe.

We used to go down to farm and dad would get on a
stack of hay, and I'd ride the horse and we'd make
hayshocks together. It wasn't easy to pile them up, they
were plenty heavy. I'd watch him gathering the hay and
tying it up with vines. Rope was no good. "Too small,"
he told me. "Rope will cut right through those shocks."

One of my earliest memories is watching him concentrating on that work, sweat coming down his face and
little twigs of hay stuck to his clothes. One after another, he'd never stop until we were done. There was a
smell to it. It was a little bit like the way greens smell
after they've been mowed. I'd help him until I'd get
tired, then I'd lay down on the pile of shocks. Some of
that hay always got inside my collar and it'd make me
crazy till we got home. We'd make I don't know how
many stacks, and then we'd have to haul some home to
feed the animals.

My dad was a Bible teacher, too, and I don't think he
ever missed a Sunday. Never sick. He didn't like doc-
tors, and he especially didn't like anyone to touch his
head. He'd take me to the barbershop, which he hated
more than I did, and he'd tell that barber, "Hurry up and
get this over with." If you came up and touched his hat,
you had a fight on. People respected him, I can tell you
that.

But one thing about my dad, he was a haughty man.
He didn't want anybody getting too close. I was always
closest to my mother, Laura. All us kids were. You
wouldn't think so, though. My mother was forty-seven

when I was born, so by the time I got to know what a momma was, she was an old gray-haired lady.

Still, she was strong. Christ, she was strong. She could put a barrel of flour in the wagon—and you know a barrel of flour weighs 195 pounds and is hard to get hold of. I remember I'd dig potatoes, two bushels to a sack. Two bushels of potatoes weighs pretty good, but my mother would pick up a sack and throw it over her shoulder. I'd say, "Aw, mom, you should let Homer help you," but she just went right ahead. I think she could have thrown me up there on top of one of those sacks and not felt the difference.

I admired that kind of strength, the kind that lets you do things nobody expected you to do. I was lucky, I inherited my size from my dad's family and my strength from my momma's. We were all so big-bodied, it was just natural to go after things that let us use our size and strength.

My momma had something else, too. She was very smart. She didn't get to go through grade school. She was oldest and her mother died and then she had to look after the rest of them. She had the kind of smarts you get from living hard, but learning from it. She was someone who had what you call front- and hindsight. People in Ashwood would come over for a visit, and then it would turn out they wanted to know what she thought of how this farm was being run, or whether it was a good idea to go into that line of business. She didn't talk an awful lot, but when she did, it was always common sense. She didn't tolerate foolishness. She once told me, "Sam, if you are ever going to bring me flowers, do it while I'm living, not after I'm dead."

That included taking us kids down a notch if she thought we needed it. I once asked her if she thought I would ever amount to anything, and she said, "If you keep hitting golf balls against my roof, you won't!"

With six kids, there was a lot of love to divide up. The times when I got closest to her were when I used to comb her hair. She just loved me to fool with it. It was gray with little black strands in it, but she wore it long. I got to the point where I could plait it, and she would sit there all day and make lunch while I fooled with her hair.

I wanted to bring her to Florida with me once, but she wouldn't go far in a car; it'd make her sick, she said. Her sister had twenty kids, fourteen or fifteen living. Her youngest kids were younger than some of her grandkids. One of her little devils would look up at an older nephew and say, "You call me uncle!"

My momma told her I wanted to take her to Florida, and my aunt said, "That's real nice," but she said it in such a way . . .

When the time came and I told momma to start getting her things together, she said, "Oh, you know I'd be sick before we got twenty miles."

I said, "Here, mom, I'll give you a can and you can sit in the back and just let 'er go." She'd never seen the ocean so I told her I'd get her a place by the ocean and she could go and put her feet in it every day.

"Oh," she'd say, "that'll be nice." But later she said, "It wouldn't be right."

I'd say, "Mom, you got Jesse and Homer here, they can look after the place."

She kept weaseling out, and I told her she was missing out on some nice warm sunshine. I laid her out a whole pretty picture. But then her sister said, "You still going to Florida?"

In the end I just couldn't get her to come with me.

She died in '40—she was seventy-five. My dad also died at seventy-five.

My brothers and sister and I were close, I suppose, but after we grew up we never got together hardly, unless somebody died. They were kind of scattered around. But if one hollered uncle, we'd still all come running.

There was a big difference in our ages. I was the last and the next oldest was three years before me, so I was "left-over" you might say. I wasn't my mother's favorite of the five kids. I'd say to her, "Pop's favorite is Homer and yours is Jess."

And she'd say, "Oh, son, now you know we care just as much for one as for the other."

And I said, "No. I know every parent has a favorite son or daughter and they cater to them a little more than the others."

"Aw, now, you shouldn't say that."

"Well, Jesus, it's cut and dried. It sticks there like a sore thumb. Homer doesn't treat dad up or fuss at him, but that's because he doesn't even know pop's around. And meanwhile pop thinks the sun comes up and goes down with him."

Homer was next to oldest in the family and twelve years older than me. He went around the world a couple times, and every now and then he'd send a postcard. Pop would read that thing about a dozen times.

He never had any trouble with his name, but the rest of us changed around a lot. Welford hated his name, so we called him Pete. Jenny's real name was Janet but nobody ever called her that. Jesse, who's a fine golfer and also became a pro, was always known as Jess. My nephew Jesse, known to golf fans as J. C. Snead, who followed in my footsteps on the PGA tour, also liked to be called J. C. My dad was Harry Gilmer, but he didn't like G., so they called him H. J.

I didn't like "Sam" either.

My sister said, "So what you want to be called, if you don't like Sam?"

I said, "I like 'Jack.' "

She said, "Oh, 'Jackson?' That sounds like a fool."

So that was the end of that.

Actually, Jenny practically raised me. She always believed I was special. She told me I could do anything I set my mind to. She really believed in me. She's still alive and eighty-four. Lyle died at sixty-eight of emphysema. Homer died on his birthday at eighty-three.

The youngest kid in a family has to be a little sharper than the oldest. You know how it is, the older ones saying, "Get out of the way, kid," and booting you around. You just want to run up and kick them on the shins. My brothers and I were so far apart in age we never really did much together. When I got into my early teens we sometimes played golf a little bit. Jess and I would play Lyle and Homer. Jess and Homer were pros already. But pretty soon I could beat their best ball, and then they didn't want to play with me any more.

I'd take Jess as a partner because he had a strength

in his arms that gave him a hell of a wallop. But I could see that his ball would always duck hook. It didn't look like he could ever hit the thing straight. I developed the same problem in the middle of my career and had the devil's time trying to lick it. Strength? Jess once hit this cow right between the eyes with his fist, nearly floored her. She horned him, and he just turned around and popped her. Following my dad, Jess was engineer at The Homestead for fifty years. They were putting a pipe together once, a big old metal thing you usually need a wrench for, and he just picked it up with his hands and fitted it together.

Lyle was the only one to take a drink and the only one to smoke. Watching him made me decide never to drink, not even wine or beer, and not to smoke. I'd carry him cartons of cigarettes like I was carrying armloads of firewood. He had emphysema, and still he smoked! Finally it killed him.

Homer wound up an electrician, but he was always my hero big brother. He was a star at every kind of sport, and I wanted to be just like him. He was mainly interested in the radio, which was at its peak around that time, the late 1920s, early thirties. He once built his own radio. He had worked with a carpenter when he was a boy, so he could build his own box. When I was a kid he had me running all over the place to get those cylinder-shaped Quaker Oats boxes so he could wrap coils around them.

He took the microphone from a telephone and suspended it with rubber bands, and we had our own radio station. It was like magic. The whole family wanted to be on the radio, so we all hauled out our musical instruments. I played banjo then. Used to play here and there for square dancing to help pick up cash when things got tight. I was a bugler in the Scouts and then learned to play trumpet. Later I played with the guys at the Poplar Hotel, just for fun.

My whole family was musical, and I picked it up. I don't know one note from the other. I could play in B-flat, sure, but that's because the horn is a B-flat instrument. But if they played in the key of C I couldn't follow. I could harmonize with them but I couldn't do the lead. If I played in B-flat I could play almost anything, as long as I knew the tune.

My mother and all her brothers played instruments of different kinds. Their father had been a fiddle maker. My mother played guitar, but her brother, Uncle John, he could play the organ, piano, fiddle, banjo, guitar—anything but a wind instrument. One sister was an opera singer, but she died early.

We'd all get together and play at once, the big old family band. We had more fun doing that stuff! Lyle was the only one of my brothers who couldn't play. Homer said to Lyle, "Why is it that the rest of us can all play something but you can't do anything?"

Lyle said, "You give me three or four drinks and I can sing like hell!"

Homer decided that with all this musical background and with his interest in electronics he might be best off trying to make a better life for himself by getting out of the hills and learning radio for real. He worked hard and saved up and went to learn radio at a school in

Pittsburgh. After school he worked in a steel mill and met a boy there whose dad was a fighter, and told Homer, "You look like you could do a little fighting."

Homer said, "No, I've got this radio thing I want to do."

The father asked if Homer would work out with his son, who he hoped would be a fighter too. Homer said okay and went ahead and did it, but the father noticed Homer was pulling his punches and was blocking the boy more than he was going at him. So the old man pulled Homer over. "Look, I want to know if my son is going to be a fighter or not. I see you pulling your punches and I want you to stop it. He and me both have to know the truth right now, yea or nay. It will give us peace of mind. No hard feelings to you or anything."

Homer said, "But your son is a friend of mine. I wouldn't do that to him."

The old man said, "Do it."

So Homer clipped the son with a left hook, and down he went. It was over in a second.

"Jesus," the old man said, "did you hit him!"

So he convinced Homer to start working with him a little bit as a fighter. Homer started doing some fighting, small time, and did all right. I think he was proud of the way he performed in the ring. He was tough and he was big and he got a lot of attention.

But then one day the old man told Homer they were bringing a ringer in, a real pro. The old man told Homer the time had come for him to decide whether or not he wanted to become a fighter. Homer said he wasn't sure. So the old man said, "Okay then, quit. Tell them you've had enough. If you don't, this guy will cut you up and I don't want to see it happen. You might kill him if you landed one, but as the competition gets better, the harder it will be to land one. You're good, you might even knock his head off, but I don't think you have the experience."

I don't think Homer took that too well. I'll never forget the way his face got when he told us all about it later on. He quit and came home and began work as an electrician. However, he did put a punching bag up on the back of the smokehouse and would go at it sometimes. It sounded like a drum. Boy, he could hit that thing.

Sometimes my mother would get tired of the racket and have to call Homer in to give her a hand around the house. She didn't do much farmwork, but it was a lot just cooking for our bunch. The rest of us worked day and night to keep that farm going. We had chickens, pigs, turkeys and an old sheep, an old ewe. That damn sheep, she knocked me down once, and just as fast as I'd get up she'd knock me down again. My dad caught her and rubbed her nose up against the barn wall.

I'd go down after hay with the wagon, that ewe'd go along too with a bunch of dogs. Well, those dogs would get into a fight with other dogs and she'd just be in there left and right. And she didn't care which dogs she butted either. Most sheep, they'd just lie there and let the dogs tear them apart, but not her.

We'd get flour by the barrel, put up all the beans, tomatoes, corn and potatoes we'd grow on our six acres. We'd kill three or four hogs a year. I started off shooting them, then got to the point where I'd quarter them. I'd trim 'em up and salt 'em down, put 'em in a sack and hang 'em in the smokehouse.

We'd make apple butter, forty-five gallons at a time. It took two or three barrels of apples that had been peeled and cut—a chore that took two or three people all day. You'd start early, put it on maybe seven o'clock in the morning, and you didn't take it off until about three in the afternoon. You'd have a big stirrer and have to stir it all the time, all the time. We all did it. It was backbreaking work and not very interesting but we all liked sitting around afterward, slathering up some bread with it and putting it away.

The only time I didn't much like was Christmas. I wasn't able to give everybody presents, on account of we were so poor. We didn't get much either. I'd go down and play with the toys the other kids got. After that I disliked Christmas, although I participate in it with my own wife and two kids.

The only part of Christmas I liked was going to cut the tree. Sometimes it was just one of those old bull pines, but we always had a tree. I knew where all the best ones were because I spent so much time in the hills. With my brothers so much older than me and all, I grew up pretty much as a wild boy. I'd go up into the hills with my gun, trapping and shooting—I could throw a stone one hundred yards, and accurately.

When I got into fifth grade I got a trap iron and I went up to the woods every day, it didn't matter what the weather was. I'd go up one side of the Alleghenies and down the other. I'd catch wildcat, fox, rabbits and weasels.

A lot of times I'd catch a couple of skunks and I wouldn't go to school that day. My mother would smell me coming. "Don't you come in this house," she'd say. "Go up in the garden there and take your clothes off and bury them."

I'd sell the pelts. We didn't get too much for them; you could make better money catching hawks. I caught hawks with a five-foot wingspan. I'd put some fresh meat in the trap—the delights we'd call them, the liver or a piece of gut. I'd put a trap up in a tree and hawks would come right down on them. I'd cut off the heads and take them down to the courthouse, where they'd pay seventy-five cents apiece for them. They were predators, you see, so it was fine to kill them.

Kids who live in the city and never hunted, trapped or fished or worked with farm animals . . . boy, they don't know what they're missing. I'll tell you something else that's fierce: I had a pet buck deer. I kept it tied for a while near our house, and dogs would come over to fool with it, but it could just tear a dog all to pieces with its horns, and the dogs soon left it alone.

It would be great for every kid in the city to experience that instead of sitting up there in the slums, with nothing to do but steal or break into things. You never heard of any crime or stuff like that down where I come from. There's so much crime now, and they've got guns and bombs and dynamite. And cocaine. When I was a kid and they talked about people taking dope, I'd think of a Chinaman down in a cellar somewhere smoking a pipe. I asked my grandson recently if there was any kind of dope going around. He said, "Yup." This is in *grade* school. When I was growing up the only time you got dope was, if you got sick, they'd shoot you with something.

Well, I say there was no dope, but there sure was moonshine. In those days with hardly any money around and the Volstead act in effect, the fastest way for a mountain boy to make a dollar was to brew up some mountain lightning. I hated the stuff, just like I stayed away from all liquor all my life. It just wasn't for me.

Those moonshiners were always at war with the police and with revenue agents. In all my days in the hills with wildcats and bears and everything else, I can tell you that my greatest danger was stumbling onto a hidden still somewhere. I came this close to taking a load of buckshot more than once.

It WASN'T LONG before I got hooked on a different kind of shooting. You guessed it. My earliest memory of golf was when I was seven or eight and I watched my brother Homer warming up his swing in the cow pasture. I used to shag balls for him. Even so, he didn't pay much attention to me. He wouldn't let me touch his clubs. So I took an old buggy whip and cut it off, then attached an old clubhead to the end. It wasn't anything you might call a club, but, man, you could just sock a ball from here to yonder with it.

One Sunday I whaled a rock through the window of the Baptist Church while the service was on, and that singing stopped awful fast. They never found out who did it, but I was sure *someone* knew. Years later, in 1949, I bought a pipe organ for that church, and only the Lord knew it was my penance.

Though I shot fine with that old buggy whip, I wanted me something more like Homer's club. So I got the idea of cutting a stick out in the woods. I'd knife-trim it down, take the knots off and leave about twelve inches of bark on for a grip. I attached an old head, and I figured I was ready to play Homer. I got my butt beat. Also, the clubs wouldn't last long before they'd break.

My real introduction to golf was from this black boy, Frank Underwood. We called him "Stetson." He could play a French harp like you never heard. That old jaw would bellow out—you know how some horn players, their cheeks will puff out? He would play, and his brother would play guitar, and I'd go listen to them.

Now, the rule at The Cascades was: you had to weigh eighty pounds before you could get your caddy badge and carry bags. I don't know how that rule started, but I can tell you it didn't last too long. I weighed seventy-five and I was a little thin for my height. But I had good arms and thin strong legs.

Well, Stetson could see this, and one day he says, "Come on, let's go caddy."

I went along but didn't tell my mother for fear she'd say no. At The Homestead they took a picture of me with this little bag; it wasn't no bigger than a cup, it had maybe five clubs in it. I had the strap over my head on the other shoulder and I was carrying it like a water-melon.

While I was waiting I fooled around hitting balls in the yard there. A lady came in and put a whole lot of dimes and nickels and pennies in my hat and, man, I thought I was the richest person in the world.

When I got home, though, I got my fanny really tanned. I cried and showed my take and said, "Look, ma, I got all this money for caddying."

She said, "I don't care. You had me worried sick. You're going to git it!" And boy, she whopped me good.

It turns out that she had been looking for me all over the town like an old cow looking for a calf. Ashwood wasn't more than a few buildings, but not too many people had phones. Nobody had seen anything of me, so she just kept looking and looking for me. The neighbors said later that she was bawling because she thought one of the moonshiners had plugged me.

"Next time, young man," she said, "you tell me when you're going on down there."

You see, she figured out that I was going to be headed down there a whole lot.

Here I am, not 10 years old, but already caddying, and already wearing a predecessor to my Palmetto. Credit: Gleneagles Country Club, Delray Beach, Florida.

There aren't many pictures of my family from when I was
growing up. But this photo of the Hot Springs Fire Department
shows my father, Harry (far left), and two of my brothers, Jesse
(third from left) and Homer (last wearing t-shirt on the right).

That's me, second from the left in the front row, on the football
team at Valley High School. Credit: Gleneagles Country Club.

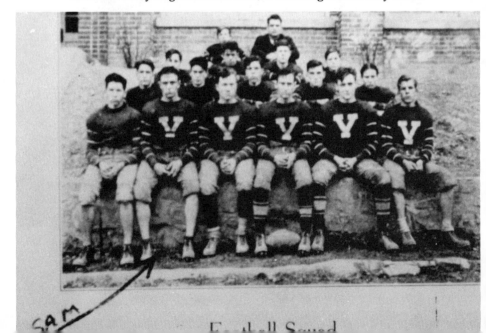

The face has changed, but the swing has stayed the same. My follow-through at age 24 in 1936 at the Greenbrier. Credit: Courtesy Tom Nichols.

Sam King and Henry Picard (leaning on clubs) watch a drive hit by me (right), age 25, at my first British Open in 1937.
Credit: Acme.

People kidded me about being a hillbilly, but that image helped fix me in the public's mind. This publicity shot was put out by The Greenbrier. Credit: Bill Wasile—Greenbrier.

Listening to a speech in my hillbilly get-up. Credit: Gleneagles Country Club.

Showing the ropes to the new generation. Credit: Gleneagles Country Club.

Chapter 2

YEARS LATER WHEN I was a pro I was challenged by a cattle rancher by the name of Tomeau. He waved around a lot of dough, which got my attention. Tommy was determined to beat me, so I took him up on it. It didn't take too long before you could see he didn't have a chance, even when I gave him the advantage of a stroke a hole. But he didn't seem to care. This guy wanted my hide one way or another and was willing to part with some cash on the way to doing it.

We tried some creative handicaps to bring us together. I gave him two strokes on all par-5 holes and one stroke on the rest, and he lost. Then I gave him two strokes on every hole more than 400 yards, and one on the rest. No good. I even agreed to play him with nothing but a 3-wood on every shot from driving to putting, and *still* he was left cussin' in Spanish and peeling off bills in my direction. I felt sorry for him, he was so determined to beat me.

That was when an old memory came to me. I went back in my mind forty years to the day I was watching Homer out in the pasture whomping 300-yard drives. I wanted to use his clubs but he wouldn't let me touch them, so I climbed up into the hills and found me one of those good straight swamp maple limbs and cut me one just the right length, with a knot at the bottom for a head.

"Tommy," I told Tomeau, "I've got a game for you that you may be able to win, and maybe not. I'll play you with nothing but a wedge and an old stick."

"What kind of a stick?" he wanted to know. It didn't take me long to hike out into the woods, cut a tree limb and whittle it up just like I did when I was a kid. It was nothing to look at, but even after years of using steel shafts I thought that branch felt fine. Tommy thought I was crazy, especially after he tried it out. He couldn't do any better with that stick than one of his cows could do kicking a football.

"The game's on!" he yelled. "It's hunting season!"

He was yelling in a different way when he saw me use the branch to smack that pill onto the fairway. I beat him again, with a respectable 76. Finally he had enough. And that was the end of the great Cuban challenge.

I wasn't about to slide that branch into my bag, but it did put me in mind of the time when a stick just like it was the only equipment I owned. People think growing up in the hills was a handicap I had to overcome. In a lot of ways it gave me a big advantage that has lasted me to this day. Just like with that stick, I'd had to overcompensate for just about everything: sticks for clubs, acorns for balls. When I finally got my hands on the real things, the regulation stuff seemed like a dream.

I found that everything I had learned in the woods and around my house could be adapted in one way or another to boost my game. All I did was remember the skills I'd picked up. How to aim. How to slam. How to reckon strategy. How to use psychology on your opponent, knowing that if you don't go out and get him he's going to take a bite out of you. And I realized I had one other skill that's just as important . . . I had learned to do it all just as quick and as quiet and as hard as could be, and to just keep doing it again and again. I figured everything out for myself. The things I figured out became the "Snead style" that people talk about.

There was no television when I was a boy, and we couldn't have afforded one if there was. So I was outside all the time, running and playing and tracking through the woods. I used to steal an old shotgun and take it to hunt squirrels. I could hardly lift it up to aim. I also made my own bows and arrows and gravelshooters—some people call them slingshots. I got to where I was pretty accurate with them. I'd use them to shoot birds out of the cherry trees, or else they'd get up there and eat them all.

Though I've rounded out later in life, I was a skinny kid. Even when I got to high school I had such long skinny legs, the kids called me "Spider." But that didn't mean I wasn't strong.

One of my jobs was to cut up logs for the furnace. I cut all the wood for winter with a one-man or a two-man cross-cut saw, working either one of them all by myself. I'd pile the logs outside the house, and I can still remember going out in the winter to split those logs. I loved cutting wood in the winter because you didn't get so hot then. Cutting wood every day gave me powerful hands and shoulders.

People have always told me my limberness is one of

the keys to my success. They're right. As I get older I see a lot of the guys who started with me turning into old men. Their biggest problem is that they don't want to move around anymore. You can't stop moving. You've got to be out there playing, every day if possible. The older you get, the more important that daily round becomes.

But the urge to do that round is something that was planted in me when I was a boy. Running around in those hills gave me muscle tone that helped me last years longer than most other guys. Part of it was that if I didn't feel toned, I just didn't feel right.

When I was growing up in Ashwood our nearest neighbor was miles away, and there weren't any kids nearby who were my age. That, along with my brothers being a lot older than I was, meant that I spent a lot of time doing things by myself.

No matter what I was doing, whether it was chores or hunting or whatever, I was usually by myself. It wasn't until years later at Valley High School in Hot Springs that I began to play on teams. Even then, I didn't like it much. I preferred relying on myself. When you play golf, you're not just playing against your opponent, you're playing against yourself. You've got to do better every single game, or else your score starts to rise right there.

I loved to swim. I could swim the length of a pond and back underwater. One day I met a bunch of kids and I wanted to give them a good show, so I did every kind of swan dive, back-flip and somersault that I could think of. My legs that night felt like they were numb.

Lots of times afterward when my sciatica got bad I thought I must have done something to the nerve right then. But at that age my nerves felt like they were made of steel.

They needed to be if I was to catch hawks and skunks and such. I used to go down to the river and catch trout with my hands. It's not hard if you know how to do it. They hide under rocks and logs and all you need to do is to reach under carefully and feel. They lay right still if you don't jerk your hands. Many a time in later years when I got the "yips" putting, I'd think about reaching out for those trout and that would help my hands move smoothly.

With the trout, if you move slow and gentle you can rub their bellies. They like that. You work up to where you can just feel the fins and then you grab 'em. I suggest thinking twice before you try this method. One day I was feeling under there and I noticed that this one felt a little rougher than usual. Anyway, I waited until he was nice and still and I grabbed him. But what do I pull up but a water moccasin! Good thing I had a good tight hold on that snake. If he'd bit me, that would have been the end of this golfer right there. Plenty of times afterward I'd be gripping a club in a tense moment in a tournament, and I'd think of that water moccasin and I'd choke that club to death. Anyway, that cured me from fishing like that for a while. Then I came up with the idea of making a snare with a piece of screen wire, and I'd reach down there and grab 'em with that.

The water moccasin wasn't the only thing I narrowly survived. I used to have a hell of a time throwing rocks at hornets' nests. The trick was to get close enough to knock it out of the tree or under the roof or wherever they happened to be, but also to keep yourself far enough away to get a running head start on all those mad hornets. You knew damn well you were going to get stung sooner or later, but I got it down to where I could get pretty close without those things catching me.

Snakes and bees weren't the only wild things that had something to teach me. I seemed to get in a fight with every new kid that came along. I don't think I ever started one, but when I saw them coming I let go the first hit. I didn't care where it hit, so long as it hit. That stopped a lot of them—but not all of them. Kids there could chew tobacco and spit ink. We'd get into fights and somehow I'd always get the finger pointed at me. I got so many whippings in school that I kept that principal in exercise.

Once I was playing marbles with my three brothers and some kids their age. I was a good shooter. I had a shoebox full. Sometimes I'd use a ball bearing as my shooter. Usually we'd play all-you-can-knock in an oblong ring with the marbles in the center. I learned that if you found two marbles sitting close together and hit right between them, you could knock both of them out. Once I did that with my ball bearing and one of these kids started yelling, "No doubles, no dubs!"

I hollered "No!"

Now, this kid knew I liked to hold my winnings in my left hand when I played. I liked the feeling of all those marbles in there. Anyway he saw my hand full of marbles, so he leaned over and knocked them all over the ground.

Well, I clobbered him. He grabbed me on the nose and his fingernails almost went right through. I'm convinced he was ready to tear my nose off. After what he'd done with the marbles, it made me want to beat his head to a pulp. I wanted to kill him.

His brother tried jumping on my back, but some of the boys pulled him off and held him until I'd worked the other kid over. When I was done I turned to those boys and said, "Turn him loose now," and then I licked the brother too.

On the way back, riding in a cart, we came up to a gate with a woman standing alongside, and there we were with black eyes and all black and blue and the woman said, "What in the world happened to you boys?"

"Oh, the horse turned over the cart," we said.

I GUESS YOU could say I looked for trouble, found it and learned to be a fighter early on. I always tried to come out on top—I learned to *compete,* and I still love it, especially when there's money in it. I don't like it when somebody tries to make a pigeon of me. I learned to compete against kids my own age when I got to high school—and boy, did I go at it.

My first sport was basketball. (I also played football and track.) It was a squall from start to finish, and I think that learning to play while kids are yelling and screaming forced me to learn how to tune them out and concentrate on just getting that ball in the basket— later, into the little hole. I was, though, the high scorer on the basketball team.

Our school was small, so it wasn't very hard to make the teams. Still, there were five of us who went from freshman to senior as the first five starters. We were The Team and we made a pretty respectable showing against teams from other high schools.

We were Baptists, but on Sunday after church we'd get out and play baseball in a hayfield. We'd just take some rocks and put them out there for second and home plate, then choose up sides. If we didn't have enough kids we'd play what you call One-Eyed Cat. You'd take a tennis ball and a picket from a picket fence, and you'd crack the devil out of that tennis ball, hoping nobody on the other side could catch it. You had to run to first base and back before they could catch it. Their job was to try to catch it and hit you with it before you got back home. If they caught your fly, or if they hit you with the ball it was their turn at bat. That game took some dodging, I can tell you. It was a lot like knocking down those hornets' nests. If the other team was thirty feet or so away, then you took a chance and started running. But if they were within ten feet, you knew they weren't going to miss you. Some of those balls could knock the stuffings out of you. I learned to think fast on my feet and to move those feet fast when I had to.

I JUST LIKED living by my own wits and depending on myself for a win. That feeling got stronger as time went on, especially after one experience when my high school principal was refereeing one of our basketball games.

We were beating the dust out of this other team, and they got the idea of coming up behind me and yanking my pants down to rattle me. They did it a couple of times, and the principal had to grab me by the collar of my shirt to stop me from killing them, I got so mad.

I could understand their wanting to haze me. What I couldn't understand is why this principal didn't tell these kids to quit it. Maybe he was trying to go out of his way to be impartial and fair, but I thought he was blinking a little too hard.

Finally I took the ball as this one kid was coming down on me, and I threw it so it bopped him on the side of his head. We went at it, and the principal threw me out of the game.

He said, "You go upstairs."

"Why don't you referee the ball game right?" I told him. "They're pulling my clothes off and tearing them."

That got me sent home for two weeks. When I told my dad about it, he came down and called that teacher out. Dad told me later that he never saw a man so nervous in his life. "He was shaking," dad said. "I think he thought I was going to hurt him. What I told him was I came up here to see about my son. He told me his side; now you tell me your side. But if what he said is right, you had no right to do what you did."

The principal thought about it, and pretty soon I was back at school, though he did make me sit out recess for a while.

For a while after that I concentrated on football and track. I could do the 100 in ten seconds the last year in high school, but we didn't have a team. I used to kick the hell out of footballs when I was in high school. I played one team and they never even returned our punt. I could kick as good as any of those college guys. I was especially good as a runner and halfback and was the team's high scorer. At that early age there were some people who pegged me as a pro prospect. But my heart finally brought me back to golf.

I ALWAYS LIKED golf. We played at Woodberry Forest in high school and we were the smallest school represented. They had sand greens; I'd never played those. The best I did was third. I did all right in the driving contests, though—finished second twice with 318 yards using a borrowed set of clubs.

Most of my practice was at home, right in our pasture. Homer practiced his drives there, and so did I for a while. I started by seeing how far I could smack rocks, measuring the distance by how many fenceposts I could hit past. I found that the best way was just to draw that stick back nice and lazy, not thinking too much about how I was doing what, but then coming down and whopping that thing over the grass. Pretty soon I found that just making it fly wasn't enough. Instead of hitting past the fenceposts, I tried to aim for the fenceposts themselves and whack them from farther and farther away. That was more like it!

One day I discovered that the quart cans my mother got tomatoes in were just over four inches across, just about the same size as a regulation golf hole. Well, I pounded a couple of those cans down in our yard and

I had me my very own golf course! I'd mow that thing every day. I'd chip around, chip around, oh, for hours. I didn't have a putter or any other specific clubs at first, just a carved stick that would work out comparable to a five-iron. We didn't have numbers on them then. They all had names. We called them a mashie, a spoon, a geeger or a cleek, a mid-mashie, or a spade, which was a seven-iron.

On my homemade course, hazards included our chicken pen and the outhouse. One of my holes was around the far side of a swamp area near the pasture. Balls were hard to come by as it was. If I hit into that swamp and had to slog in after it, I'd catch it good from my mother. So I learned real early how to keep out of bunkers and how to make tricky doglegs all in one swoop.

I'd spend every spare minute knocking balls from one field down to the other, and they'd bang up on the tin roof, and she'd come out squalling, "What are you doin'?"

My mother never encouraged me to follow my talent, so one day, after I'd gone on the circuit, I asked her, "Did you ever think I'd amount to anything?"

She said, "Yes. I always thought you would, because you were never still. You were always doing something."

The one thing I was always *doing* was playing golf. I couldn't get enough. My brother and I would hike three miles down the road to a course they had at The Cascades Hotel in Hot Springs. There were always plenty of old lost golf balls out in the woods, and we'd collect them for the home course. But the real reason to go was to get a taste of real golf. There was this old gent up there, and his job was to keep people off. We'd get to play one hole before he'd come after us and we'd have to run through the woods and come out again at another hole. We'd chip around the green and get maybe one putt before he'd catch up to us again and we had to run for it. Another problem was our equipment, if you could call a couple of green maple sticks "equipment." I'd carry some nails around in my pocket and keep putting on the cast-iron heads I'd hammered on. But sticks never lasted too long.

Though we all eventually became caddies there, Homer actually didn't golf with me much. Lyle even less. The golf partner I remember was my Uncle Billy. It all started when I was pretty small. He'd come up every Sunday morning. He'd grab me by the ear or the hair on top of my head—maybe that's what started my hair coming out—and he'd say, "Come on, damn you, we're going to pitch horseshoes." And we'd go on out to the back of the barn and pitch until my mother would call us for lunch. But once he saw me chipping around on my farmyard course, and he called out to me, "Give me that!" And so we stopped horseshoes and started chipping around holes.

I had one long down, about twenty-five, thirty yards, and then another at the other end of the yard, maybe about fifty yards. The two of us would go over and through and up and around. One Sunday he came up there with a crazy bag of all kinds of clubs, half left-handed, half right-handed, and of course all wooden shafts. So we started to play with this old bastard set. Uncle Billy would set up a ball, then whip and miss the whole damned thing. He played half left-handed for the long shots, then chipping around the yard and putting with the right-handed club.

Watching him, I had a thought. I could see he was proud of those clubs, and wanted to try them out. So I said, "Okay, how about this . . . I bet my sticks can still beat those new clubs. If I'm right, you've got to treat me to a sundae."

He said, "You're on, but on one condition. If you lose, you gotta treat me."

I was pretty sure of myself, so I jumped right into it.

On one hole I saw him swing seven times, but when I asked him what he had, he said, "Five."

I said, "Whoa, you whiffed two of them."

He said, "Boy, them was practice swings."

I said, "Yeah, but you grunted."

But it was no use. I couldn't beat him. He never seemed to be able to count higher than five. So I took him down to the drugstore and I had to buy him the biggest sundae in the place. It must have cost fifteen cents, and fifteen cents was a bite, I can tell you.

Nobody really took my golfing seriously—including me at that point. My mother thought I was going to be a tailor! I had picked up the knack of sewing pretty early on, my fingers being just right for it. When I was in high school I knew how to take in my own pants, sew on a new cuff, anything like that. I had a pair of blue serge pants once, and you could walk from here to the front door in them and the crease would be gone. So I sewed me a crease and, boy, I had the sharpest pants you ever saw. Ma said, "My God, you got a crease in those pants!"

My dad had an old overcoat, a big heavy damned thing that you could have gone to the North Pole in, and around the collar it was all kind of worn and dirty-like. I took that thing off, turned it around and sewed it back on, and it looked almost like new, and my ma said, "Son, you're gonna be a tailor."

To this day I carry a sewing kit everywhere with me. Just in case I need to sew a button on. I just like fiddling with things like that, and that goes for everything from a fishing reel right up to a bulldozer and a backhoe. I own both, and I'm still using them. They're big, but they require a careful touch or else you're over in a ditch.

I ALWAYS HAD a strong sense of making money and saving it. I had to do that if I wanted to buy anything; my father couldn't afford it. Along with the money I made trapping and hunting, I sometimes took my banjo down into town and I'd play for change on the street. If I wound up with a dollar I'd say I was doing pretty good.

But as I got older I went to work at the same drugstore where I bought that sundae for Uncle Billy. I worked for Doc Grisley, a great big stoop-shouldered guy who'd say, "Scrape those dippers, you're not pulling up any ice cream 'cause they're loaded with slush!"

I went fishing with him a couple of times; then, when I was on tour, I wrote him a letter telling him how much I'd liked him. Do you know that he kept that letter and they found it in his safe when he died?

He paid me seventy-five cents a night, and I worked three nights a week and every other Saturday and Sunday. Most of that money went for my clothes and my schoolbooks, so it didn't go very far. And that was a hardship, because I started courting a little bit then, the same pretty girl I eventually married. When I wanted to take her out I had to ask my brother to borrow what we called Old Mary, a two-wheel-braked Chevrolet with a cloth top. I guess I was about fifteen, sixteen then.

But of all the ways of making a little extra money open to kids my age, my favorite was caddying. I caddied all through my teenage years, caddied barefoot in the snow until one day my feet were frostbit and I came within an inch of losing some toes.

When I was eighteen—that was 1930—I landed a caddy job at The Cascades Hotel in Hot Springs, where I got a chance to meet and watch some fine players. I was itching to show them what I could do, but that wasn't part of my job.

After a while I got a job as club mate in the pro shop. Part of my job was maintaining clubs, putting on new wooden shafts. I had to be real careful trimming them down because if you trimmed them down too much they'd be too whippy. You'd have to feel them over, turn a little bit, trim a little bit, then feel some more. I knew how from doing my own. I'd put linseed oil and shellac on the shaft and rub it in. Man, that thing would be as slick as could be. Then I'd put on the grip and the head, and there you'd have it.

I didn't buy my first set of real clubs until 1934, when I was twenty-two. They were a set of Bobby Jones Spalding irons. It was when they first came out with steel shafts, and I just had to have them. I bought those clubs at $5, one club at a time, from the pro. I wasn't getting paid to give lessons then, but the club didn't mind if somebody wanted to slip me a dollar or two. Overall, I didn't earn enough to pay for my laundry. Every time I got five or ten dollars, I'd take it over to the pro and he'd sell the clubs to me—and not at wholesale either.

I never could understand that man. He was a good teacher and the most athletic person I ever saw around that club. He'd call people up, and if it was raining he'd take them up to the shelter house and they'd hit balls out there. But I thought he was kind of mean where I was concerned. Couldn't figure it.

He wasn't the only problem, either. This was after the big Crash and nobody could afford to play, hardly. When I'd give lessons on the side, people would come in and I had to lend them half of my own clubs so they could play. I'd charge them a dollar and a half. I'd keep just enough clubs so I could play, and got a lot of experience playing shots with unusual clubs. I learned to drive with an iron when I had to, and putt with a wedge.

I began refining my technique. I learned to think about the shot, reconnoiter the fairway and the wind and the sun; then line it up, hold still—and move in one continuous motion, just all in one piece from your feet to the tip of your fingers.

I was earning $20 a month at the pro shop now, working seven days a week, twelve hours or more each day, and trying to decide what to do with myself. I was a kid, the same age as these college kids when they graduate and just as confused, but with nothing like the family support and sure as hell with nothing like the bread. Nobody had ever told me I might get along someplace in this world. It was assumed that I was going to take some kind of laboring job just like everybody else. There was nothing wrong with that, and I had the arms and the back for it, too. But I wanted to golf like nothing else.

So there I was, working at The Cascades for not a whole lot more than lunch—a sandwich and a glass of milk—and the chance to play all the golf I wanted. Most people thought the idea of becoming a professional golfer was a little farfetched—until they saw me drive the ball.

The only thing I could do was keep hoping somebody would notice me. And before long, somebody did.

Chapter 3

I'VE BEEN ASKED what made me decide to enter The Cascades Open in 1936, especially since I'd more or less
been banished to the back of the caddyshack repairing
clubs and sweeping up. Now and then I'd go out on the
course to give old ladies a few pointers, but more often
than not the only time I got on the course was to patch
divots.

Never mind. When the hotel announced it was host-
ing an open, nobody or nothing was going to stop me
from entering. I was itching to show off my form, and the
prize money didn't look too bad, either, considering
some of the bills I'd run up.

Playing like a madman, I managed to hit a few shots
that got some whistles from the spectators. Being green
as a pea, I was still able to do just fine on raw power.
I knew a few tricks, but I knew next to nothing about
the fine points. I didn't have to, then. At the ninth hole
I hit a drive that must have gone more than 300 yards.
Billy Burke won with a 70, but he had a run for his
money.

I was still counting the $358.66 third-place prize
money when up steps a man who introduces himself as
Freddy Martin, manager of golf at a big hotel called

48

The Greenbrier just over the border in White Sulphur Springs, West Virginia. It seemed that Freddy had heard a thing or two about some peckerwood wonder boy over at The Cascades. It so happened the day he stopped by to check the rumors, I was shooting hot as a pistol.

"You fire that ball a country mile," he said. "Where'd you get that swing?"

I told him about my course at home, and he couldn't believe it. It was the first time I'd ever told my story to anyone big, and I think I was a little proud of it. I kept jawing on about me and my brother Homer and how I made my own clubs. I showed him my set and he looked like he wasn't sure whether to laugh out loud or give the things a decent burial. But I guess he liked the way I could talk about golf, even with my mountain accent, which was ninety percent twang.

"You hit some of the longest balls I've ever seen," he told me. "How'd you like to come over to The Greenbrier and work for me as a full-fledged professional? You'll get $45 a month with room and board, and you can keep anything you make giving lessons on top of that."

The Greenbrier! Presidents and high society had nested there since before the Civil War, and the course was one of the best in the country. I was only twenty-three years old then. I kept up my relationship with The Greenbrier for over thirty years, but I still remember the way that conversation made me feel, with Freddy standing there with his arms crossed, looking me straight in the eye. It changed everything. I've thought to myself, what if he hadn't come that day, or what if I'd got the "yips" or had blasted all my shots off the map like I did in my first major tournament a few months later? Would somebody else have come along? I suppose it's foolish to think of such things.

Anyway, I sure didn't think about it at the time. I ran the three miles home that night, packed up a couple of white shirts, some gray wool pants and a sweater, and hopped into Old Mary while it was still dark out the next morning.

Birds were still singing when I hit the first tee. I had no idea what a fool I looked like, especially to the name pros on the staff who had a whole golfing wardrobe. All I knew was that it was my time to start getting along, and I was fierce to play anybody they gave me.

Steve Gagan, head pro at the time, took me by the arm and sort of suggested that I might want to take a few days to get introduced to the courses there before I started showing other people how to play them.

I had no idea, but Freddy Martin had come back to Greenbrier singing my praises. It was his plan that the club should get up the funds to send me out as a touring pro. One of the most important folks he'd have to convince was one Alva Bradley, a grouchy little rooster with a big belly and a nasty temper. Bradley was president of the Cleveland Indians baseball team, but, more important, he was on the board of directors of the Chesapeake and Ohio Railroad Company, which owned The Greenbrier.

You could tell whenever he was coming off the 18th hole because he'd always be swearing and raising a fuss—it was all he could do to break 100 and he had a habit of blaming it on whatever pro he was working with at the time. Besides his problems in hitting around his paunch, that man had a fearful slice that looked incurable.

"Steer clear," the other pros warned me, and I took their word for it. So it was an accident that I encountered Mr. Bradley out on the fifth hole one morning. I was practicing my drive off the tee while Mr. Bradley's party was finishing up their putting. Well, a little breeze caught my drive and it sailed down all 335 yards of that hole and smacked Bradley right in the seat of his pants. It was like something out of a Laurel and Hardy movie the way that man jolted up. He was hopping mad, and that's the truth.

I was so rattled I just loped down there as he was coming up to get me. "If I could just explain, sir," I tried to say, but he was ready to let me have it.

"You hit me!" he was hollering. "Why don't you watch where you're hitting your goddammed ball?"

"I'm danged sorry," I said, "but I can explain—"

"What's your name?" he demanded, and as shook as I was, I told him I was the new pro.

"We'll see about that!" Bradley bellowed, and he stomped off to the clubhouse. I didn't know what to do, I figured it was all over for me.

Bradley, he went right to Freddy Martin and ordered him to pack me back to Dogpatch, or wherever I'd come from. Freddy tried to stand up for me, but there was no use in that. Bradley thought I'd had no manners and had tried to play through an occupied green. I tried to explain that he'd been hit by my tee shot, but nobody would believe it. Luckily I had my caddie there, and he took my part.

"It was Mr. Snead's first shot," he explained to L. R. Johnson, who was managing director of Greenbrier. Bradley wanted my scalp, but Johnson was ready to hear all sides.

"That's ridiculous," Bradley said. "It's impossible for anyone to drive that green. It hasn't happened in the fifteen years I've been playing here."

Martin must've seen this was the last chance to save his pro, so he started telling them what he'd seen me do over at The Cascades Open. Furthermore, he said he thought I should be reinstated and backed for a run at the big time.

Bradley was outraged, but I could see then that I might have one last chance. "Mr. Bradley," I said, "if you'll give me another chance I'll take you out on the course tomorrow morning and prove it to you." I think by then he was almost as curious as he was mad, so the next morning he came out with me.

I pulled out the stops for him and you should've seen his eyes popping out of his head. I let out all the shaft I could, and swung hard enough to rupture myself. My balls were flying all over Greenbrier that morning, and just for good measure I replayed my 335-yard drive onto the green at the fifth, just like I had the day before.

Bradley sang a different tune then. Right there he asked me to be his personal instructor for the rest of the season and told me he was sure I'd be famous someday.

We began working together right away. I could see what his problem was, and I showed him a few things that added yards to his drives and knocked his score down into the 90s. I tried to teach him my stroke, and that forced me to think about it and to break it down into parts.

Except the real secret was, there were no parts. It was pretty much all one motion. I told him that I'd hum a tune and use the rhythm of the music to time my swing so it came out naturally. I also realized that I led with my hips, and I used my feet as anchors for every shot I made. I found that if I rolled my right foot just a little bit and let the power come from there, I was about as rooted as an old pine tree and could put that power right behind the ball.

When Bradley started playing regularly in the low 80s, he looked like he was ready to kiss me. "Take this hundred dollars and buy some real clubs," he said. But I used the cash to buy some higher-toned clothes like the other pros had. I also bought a car of my own. It was a jalopy but it would do for what I was planning. Since Freddy Martin had said he wanted to send me out on the PGA tour, I got it in my head to try my luck at some more open tournaments. There were a couple in our area, mostly at resorts for folks from the Washington region.

The nearest was at Huntington, West Virginia, but I had already missed it for 1935. I went back, though, and in the end I won the West Virginia Open seventeen times, right up to 1972, by which time I was in the seniors but still shooting my age. Matter of fact, from age sixty to right now I've shot my age at least once every year.

Back in 1935, though, and looking to show off, I heard that the course record down at Guyon Country Club was a 69 held by PGA champ Denny Shute. That struck me as a little high, and thinking I could better it, I told Freddy Martin, who drove me over.

You should've seen the crowd of locals who turned out to razz me for thinking I could beat their local hero. I kept my mind on the ball, just like I did back at Valley High School at those crowded basketball games, and wound up the morning with a 67. I was so hot to show these folks just exactly who they were giving the needle to, so I went out again in the afternoon and broke my own record, shooting a 66.

A guy came up to me then, and shoved a book into my hands. Funny-looking thing, I thought, it's just got a bunch of names in it, no printing.

I learned then and there what an autograph book was. I got to see a few in my time, but that first one made me feel like I'd been struck by lightning.

AFTER THAT, FREDDY decided he could have some fun with me, especially since word was starting to get around about the kid from the hills who could hit meteors. He lined up an exhibition match, pairing me with Johnny Goodman, who'd won the 1933 U.S. Open. The two of us went up against national amateur champ Lawson Little and the 1931 U.S. Open winner, Billy Burke.

There were plenty more of those autograph books there that day, but none of them was for me. It didn't bother me, though. I figured my time would come. Anyway, it would come if I could keep hitting the way I'd done. This was my first chance to play with not just pros but national champions. By the time it was my turn to shoot my hands were shaking, I was so edgy. The other pair had shot first, and they had done real good. This here is the end of the line, I started to think as I teed up and started my address. But then I told myself to hush. I thought of all the drives I'd made in my life, and how happy I was being a pro and playing with the best. And I especially thought how great it felt to watch those little birds go flying down the fairway. I think I even started daydreaming a little bit as I was swinging, just humming and enjoying the day when all of a sudden I heard the crowd gasp, and I realized they were gasping at my hit!

My ball flew a good 280 yards, 25 or 30 past anything the other boys had hit. They all had a "not too bad" look on their faces, but I don't think they had any idea of the trouble they were in.

My second shot landed in tall grass at the top of the green, about 45 feet from the pin. The other fellas landed theirs right on the green in two, with easy two-putts for par 4. Figuring I'd need enough firmness to hop out of that grass, but then roll nice and easy the rest of the way, I fished out an iron and spanked that baby right out of the grass and into the cup for a birdie.

Things kept going my way that day, and at the end of the match I led with 68, 70 for Burke, 71 for Little, and 73 for my partner Goodman. He and I shared the prize, but I don't think he believed it.

The mood on the day of my first professional win was

more of shock than congratulations. In those days rounds in the 60s were considered minor miracles, and naturally everybody but Freddy Martin and Mr. Bradley thought my score must have been some kind of fluke.

I couldn't understand it at first. Somebody explained to me that it was embarrassing for the star guests to be shown up so bad. But, hell, we weren't playing any kids' game here. They shot their best and so did I. You see, it wasn't so much that they had lost, but that they had lost to a green kid out of the hills. Later on, when I was "one of them," we were all buddy-buddy and it was okay. I understood it. But at the time, everybody thought I was a smartass with a sack of luck and no manners.

I PLAYED MY first West Virginia Open the next year at Huntington, and it was raining cats and dogs. I went to town. A little rain wasn't going to bother me none. They had one tee that had no grass on it at all, just dirt. With that rain and all, it got pretty sloppy. You'd just sink into that mud, and once you'd sunk a little, you'd just have to work your feet down into that muck to get a firm stance. I couldn't turn as much but I made a little more cock at the wrist.

I ended up shooting 65 while nobody else in the tournament broke 80. But along the way something happened that affected the way I played the rest of my life.

At the ninth hole some guy came up to me and said, "Mr. Snead, they're moving up to the grass out of all this dirt, you better move up there, too."

So I did, and played the hole from the grass. But then

up comes Fred Burns, who says, "What the hell do you think you're doing up here?"

I told him about the guy who told me to get up on the grass, but Burns said, "That guy had no business telling you that. You're going to get yourself disqualified."

I said, "Wait just a minute. I can prove that you and everybody else has been playing off the grass, and every hole, too. I only played the ninth off the grass."

So you know what they did? They threw out that whole round. Seems they didn't like me because I just came in there from Virginia. Virginians and West Virginians didn't get along much. They still don't. Even the cops hate each other.

So there it was, my first big tournament and somebody was out there trying to give me the needle. Whenever I see that now, I speak right up, just the same as I did then, and I tell 'em, "Knock it off."

Actually, it wasn't the first time it had happened. When Freddy Martin noticed me at The Cascades Open, it was during a time when I was getting shuttled back and forth between pro shops at The Cascades and another hotel they owned down the road, The Homestead. I had entered an open tournament there when I was twenty or twenty-one, and I was actually leading the tournament when I got the needle.

Word was that a man by the name of Ingalls, who was president and big honcho at The Homestead, didn't want me to win. He thought it wouldn't give him any publicity. He wanted Henry Picard or one of those other big-name guys to win.

So Freddy Gleim, head pro at The Homestead—he

made the pairings and decided he was going to be playing with me. He had no right to do that, actually, but
there you are.

Soon I'm leading the tournament by three shots. On
the second tee Gleim interrupted me and said, "How do
you expect to play golf with your left elbow coming up
like that?"

I followed his advice and kept my elbow down, but
it was unnatural for me. I never hit the ball very high.
For me to keep my elbow up, I'd really have to snap it.
I thought that if Gleim said I should do it, then I should
do it. So I kept that elbow down and, I tell you, that ball
went halfway up a mountain. I ended up with an 8 on
that hole, which knocked me right out. I came in third,
shooting 80.

My brother Homer came up to me. "What the hell
happened to you?"

I said, "Ah, Gleim screwed me up."

Homer wanted to go whip him, but I said, "The hell
with him."

That pro had known just what to do. He didn't want
me to win, and Billy Burke won the tournament. I never
forgot that. I said, "Well that was a great lesson, somebody giving me the needle." But I didn't like it, because
it kept me from winning my first tournament. I would
have won easy if he hadn't done that. I never forgave
him for that.

When I went to The Greenbrier in '36, Gleim told the
boy that took my place, "Don't worry about him, he'll
never amount to anything."

So this boy who was never going to amount to anything, he won the West Virginia Professional Golfers
Association Tournament in 1936 at the ripe old age of
twenty-three. I was paired with the next two leaders
and I shot 61, which raised a few eyebrows. (I went on
to win the West Virginia PGA ten more times, the last
in 1967, the year I turned fifty-five.)

IN THE SUMMER of 1936 I was feeling pretty good, having
won both the West Virginia Open and West Virginia
PGA, but my life savings didn't amount to $300. I heard
they were having a $5,000 open up north in Hershey,
Pennsylvania, so with Fred Martin's blessing I packed
my beat-up clubs and the best clothes I had, which
weren't much, and hopped a third-class railroad coach.
    Besides the money, I hankered to see more of the
famous golfers of the day, like Walter Hagen and Bobby
Cruickshank. These men were legends to me. I had no
illusions that my West Virginia wins were going to
mean anything up against those big guns. I just wanted
to watch their style and maybe dream a little about
what I might feel like someday when I was standing in
their cleats.
    Arriving early, I found a few of the contenders getting
ready for a practice round. With my Emmett Kelly
clothes and backwoods accent I couldn't get anything
but laughs out of these guys. I was tall and gangly with
stringy black hair parted sharp on one side and slicked
over.

Finally there came a little man with a soft voice who
didn't make fun of me. "Go change your shoes, kid," he
said. "Come and shoot a round with us."

Turns out this fella was George Fazio, teacher and
pro, who I was later to play against many times, including in the U.S. Open. None of the other players wanted
to have anything to do with me, but George told them
to hush, and they did what he said.

I concentrated so hard on that ball you'd think it
would catch fire. I soon wished it had. The first shot
sliced right out of the course onto the grounds of a
chocolate factory next to the fairway. I concentrated
harder but wound up doing the same damned thing
again. I managed to keep the third one inside the
bounds of the course, but it drowned in a water hazard
below the tree. Those three shots were some of the most
unprofessional golf I'd played since becoming a pro,
and I wanted to jump into that water after my ball.

Fazio's partners wanted to throw me in. "Where the
hell did you get this guy, George?" they asked Fazio.
They already placed shots onto the fairway.

Fazio just said, "Try again, son."

I relaxed a little bit and tried not to concentrate so
hard. I knew that when I was relaxed and let my body
plan the swing, I'd get my natural winning stroke.
Around came my club and I let go a smoker.

At first they thought I'd sent another one to the chocolate factory, but Fazio had followed the path of the ball,
and he was speechless. Not only had I stayed on the
course, I'd hit on the green, about twenty feet from the
pin of a 345-yard hole.

By the time we all got down there, nobody was saying anything. They were looking from me to that ball, trying to figure out what one had to do with the other. Now I was really relaxed. I thought for a second that I'd lost the touch, but it was just nerves. Even after years of playing, I always found that the yips were my worst enemy.

My luck held again, and I finished the round with a 70, including the three unplayables at the first tee. Picard's partners couldn't find anything more to say than "son of a bitch, son of a bitch."

Word of that practice round got about pretty fast. Henry Picard, one of the champions I'd hoped just to glimpse far off, came over and kind of took me under his wing. He told me I was to be paired with another of my heroes, Craig Wood. But Picard had something else just as important to tell me.

"If you can impress Wood, you may wind up with something even more valuable than a few pointers," he said. "I talked to him about you, but don't you tell him that you talked to me. Wood is thinking of signing you for Dunlop."

Rube that I was, I'd never heard of product endorsements. The Dunlop Tire and Rubber Company was a big manufacturer of golf balls. Wood was one of their reps, and he was on the lookout for some hotshot to add to their stable of pros. Picard told me my signature on a Dunlop contract would mean I'd get $500, a set of clubs and two dozen balls a month. In those Depression days, that looked like a fortune to me.

As it turned out, Wood had no intention of making me

earn it easy. On the 10th hole—a par four, about 300 yards—I blew that ball up into a blind green. We came around the dogleg and saw that one ball was on the back end of the green and one short on the front of the green. Wood started walking by the front ball, assuming that the longer drive was his. But Wood's caddy piped up, "Mr. Wood, I believe this is your ball down here."

He got red clear up in his face. When he got through putting he turned to me and said, "Would you like to be with Dunlop?"

I said, "That would be great."

He said, "You'll get a contract."

It was my first tournament out of the South, and I finished a good fifth. I went back to The Greenbrier and waited for a month, but no contract came. I figured, well, they just forgot. Then the next day, sure enough, here comes the contract, and shortly after that, a check. It meant more to me than increasing my bankroll to $800. It meant I could afford to try my luck on the national PGA circuit. I'd finally have a chance to see all the places in the country I'd only heard about, and it meant I'd have a chance to measure myself against the top players in the world.

I WENT FIRST to Florida to play in the Miami Open, where I met a golfer named Johnny Bulla. Then I went over to Nassau, where I didn't play too well. A group was sitting around there—it included both Wood and Picard—and I said, "Mr. Wood, what do you think my chances are of going on the tour out to California?"

Picard answered for him: "You'd have to finish one, two or three to make expenses."

But Wood said, "I think this boy is asking whether he should stay home and teach or try for a career as a tour pro." I said he was right. Wood then said, "Why don't you give it a try? If you can't make it, I'll give you enough money to come home on."

"By gosh, you can't ask for anything better than that!" I told him.

So Bulla and I drove out there together, taking along a football player we met. He'd come out to play for North Carolina but they wouldn't take him, and now he was looking for a way back home to California. In return for a lift he agreed to pay half our gas and oil. As it turned out, he went back and became an all-American end for USC. All we knew at the time was that he was this crazy kid who could roll us out of bed in the morning so we'd go run with him.

WE WERE HEADED for the 1937 Oakland Open, and I was feeling real good, not just because I was living out a dream of mine but because I had found myself a rabbit's foot—a steel-shafted rabbit's foot to be exact. I had gotten this great Izett driver from Picard. I like to look at clubs so I'd pulled this one out of his bag. Picard saw me admiring it and said, "Go ahead, look at it. Try it and use it. If you like it, you can have it. It's too big for me."

The Dunlop driver I had—it was so whippy, hell, I could hit 300 yards with it right, left, or straight up! The Izett was a much heavier club, but, boy, did it give me control on power swings. My driving improved a lot.

It wasn't the only valuable new piece of equipment I was toting. I had been playing Leo Wallop, and we were standing on the green when he said, "Come on, Sam, I'll putt you a quarter a hole."

I said, "I don't have a putter."

He said, "Try one of mine."

In those days before regulations, guys might carry twenty-two, twenty-three, twenty-four clubs if their caddies would stand for it. Leo had a whole raft of them, and I just sorted through until I found one I liked. I picked it up and, man, did that feel good. I putted three straight aces with that one, and Leo started saying, "Now, don't fall in love with that one, that's mine. I use that."

I said, "Oh, I don't want it." But I had that Izett driver and I wanted that putter too. Later, Leo followed me into the clubhouse and said, "Hey, if you want that putter you can have it for three dollars and fifty cents."

Whoa, I had to contain myself. I turned my pocket inside out to get that money.

So now I was headed for California with my two most important clubs in the bag, putter and driver. I said to Bulla, "I heard some of the pros out there today, they split whatever they make. This way, if one of them blows up and the other lands in the money, nobody comes home broke." I called him Boovoo, he called me Jackson. I said, "Boovoo, you want to split with me?"

He said, "Hell no, Jackson, you can't play a lick."

I said, "That so? Boovoo, I'll play you five dollars every tournament from here on."

He said, "The game's on! Want to make it more?"

We stopped off at the Los Angeles Open to try our West Coast luck. Coming down to the 17th hole I'd hit a good drive, and then along comes Bulla. He had just finished up the hole and he wanted to see how I was going to do.

"Jackson," he said, "I hope you've got a six-iron."

I said, "It doesn't look like a six-iron to me."

He said, "I ought to know, I just played it."

I said, "What'd you shoot?"

He said, "Never mind that."

I hit a seven-iron 170 yards with no problem. I whipped it right in there about ten feet right below the hole. They had some real small greens there and I saw that if I'd used a six-iron, I'd have been right over the green.

I won $600 and he didn't win a nickel, and I said "Boovoo, hand over that five dollars!"

I MET FRED Corcoran early one morning at the Leamington Hotel near the Lake Merritt Club. He'd seen me play in the qualifying rounds and had invited me up to a breakfast with some touring professionals to help promote the Oakland Open. New on the PGA tour, I decided I couldn't say no to the unusual hour, but when I got to the course I found I was the first one there. It wasn't too long, though, before I saw this big bull-headed Irishman coming over to me, wearing a big colorful tie.

"Are you a golf professional?" he said.

"Yes, sir, I'm Snead."

Neither of us knew then that it was the start of a personal and professional relationship that was to survive more than a quarter century. He was tournament manager of the PGA then, and hadn't turned to personal management yet. But in the years ahead, Fred would manage the likes of Babe Ruth and Stan Musial. He had an almost infallible touch for getting the public to sit up and take notice.

As it turned out, Fred and I were the only ones who showed up for this breakfast hour exposition, so we went out to play a match together for the five hundred or so yawning local golf fans who had dragged themselves out of bed to see some would-be champions. I reminded Fred to mention the fact that I was from The Greenbrier, seeing as how I was still getting $45 a month to represent the place.

Fred and I must have given them a hell of a show, because when we got up to Oakland the following week and cracked the local paper, Speck Hammond, Walter Hagen's caddy and valet, had put a squib in the paper there, saying, "I'm picking a dark horse to win this tournament—Sam Snead, S N double-E D."

By God, I did win. And under awful conditions of wind, rain and fog. You had to send your caddy out in front before you shot because the wind would suck your ball down, and you couldn't find it right in the middle of the fairway. As we were coming down the last three holes, people started coming up the road, over the ditches, and they started lining the fairway good and close from one end to the other.

I'd never seen anything like it and was hollering, "What the hell is going on here?"

Johnny Revolta, Ralph Guldahl and another player—they were bunched up and I was a shot or two behind. I caught Revolta first. On the 12th hole he made 6 and I made 3. I dusted him, but I made like I didn't pay attention and just played on. I took the lead the first day with a 69 on a par-70 course, and topped it the next day with a 65. They told me, "Nobody shoots sixty-five on that course!"

Like always before, folks figured I was a fluke and waited for me to collapse, but I shot 67 on the third round and was tight coming in to the finish.

All of a sudden on the last three holes all these people were there. On the 17th hole the trees interlocked from one end to the other, that's how narrow it was. I took a one-iron and just drove that ball on down—it was 400 yards or more and wet. Balls wouldn't run at all. So I had a four-iron in my hand when Orville White comes running up with my pal Bulla and another guy, and he says, "You got to par to tie!"

"Jesus Christ!" I said, and proceeded to put it right up into the trees, making a bogey 5.

That left the last hole, a par 5. On the left side was a gully, and it was dark in there. Bulla said, "For God's sake, Jackson, keep it way up to the right!"

I did. On my second shot I hit a two-wood just short of the bunker. I had an eight-iron, and I played it like a wedge. All my experience playing all kinds of shots with just one club was starting to pay off. Also, that bunker lay just like the mud patch next to my pasture course, so I felt right at home. I used an eight-iron—I don't know why, I had wedges and everything else by then—but I somehow had more confidence in that eight. I zipped that thing in at four feet, and whapped it right in the hole for a birdie four.

As I was walking off the green, this photographer came running up to me. "I've gotta have your picture, you just won the tournament!"

"Just you get away from me," I said. "You're not going to take my picture, it's bad luck. You're counting chickens before they're hatched."

Just then, Freddie Corcoran came over and said, "You come out to the press tent with me, now. You just won."

I said, "Mr. Corcoran, all those other fellows are still out there."

He told me, "They'll never beat you now, boy."

So I went up there and was sitting on the table, and the photographer snaps my picture before I was ready for him. I'd never seen a flash camera before, and it scared the hell out of me—you can tell from looking at the picture. I thought I was going blind. The next day it was in all the local papers, with my name spelled SNEED.

They didn't spell it wrong for long. Within just a few days every sports columnist and golf fan had the spelling right. Playing in only my second PGA tournament I had scored 270 to win, and picked up my check for $1,200. It was more money than I'd ever seen in one place, but I knew I'd soon see five dollars more. Bulla had to cough up, and he must've been banging his head against a tree thinking about how $600 of that prize could have been his.

When things had settled down a few days later, Corcoran came over to me with a big satisfied smile on his face. "Sam, take a look at this."

It was a New York paper, and it had that picture of me sitting on that table. I was outraged. "Hey, Mr. Corcoran," I said, "how did they get my picture in New York? I ain't never been there!"

I knew nothing about wire services or any of that. But Corcoran was grinning that big old cat-eyed grin of his. He would teach me.

Chapter 4

FRED CORCORAN TELLS a story about coming into a clubhouse and seeing "Lighthorse" Harry Cooper in the corner where he had corralled two or three reporters and was laying into them.

"What the hell goes here?" said Lighthorse to the scribes, "I'm playing on this course and this goddamned Snead kid is getting all the ink. What gives?"

And one of the reporters supposedly said, "Hell, what are we supposed to write? 'Lighthorse Harry wins again'? We've got this here hillbilly to write about, and he's got more stories than you can shake a stick at."

Is that story true? The real question is, were any of Corcoran's stories true? I'll say that they all had a piece of truth in them. Fred knew how to tell a story, all right, and he knew how to get newspaper reporters to listen to them.

Fact is, the press has always been a pain in the ass to us. Sure, there were some okay reporters: Jimmy Burns, Jim Berry, Charlie Bartlett . . . but a lot of them gave us an awful time. Pressure from the public can get pretty high, especially when a lot is riding on a big tournament. But in the end every professional golfer has got to swallow the fact that without the gallery there's no big-time golf, or any big-time sport for that matter. I've always been appreciative of what side my bread is buttered on. And it was Fred Corcoran who taught me how sports and the media hold hands.

Being good, though, is always the most important thing, even if a lot of pros lose sight of that. But you can't hide your light under a bushel. After being good, the next most important thing is being noticed.

That sounds simple and natural today, with cable TV and regular TV scratching each other's eyes out to get a piece of every sport from football to bowling. And athletes going on the TV news every night giving their opinions of themselves and each other and everything from foreign policy to the weather. But it wasn't always that way. Especially not in golf. Golf was a sport for rich British guys in knickers and spectacles. Most people then thought golf was the slowest-moving sport in the world, and that folks who played it were boring. To some extent, that was true. What golf needed was a few colorful characters, and a few wheeler-dealers to make it all go.

That's why, though we really didn't realize it at the time, Fred Corcoran and I were the perfect match. We helped make golf a sport for the average Joe. Folks would say, "Hell, if that hayseed Snead can lick those rich guys, so can I!" And that helped fill up the gallery, too. During the ten years Fred worked as PGA tournament director, the value of the tour jumped from $100,000 to more than $1 million, and it's just kept going.

*   *   *

I WASN'T JUST good, I've stayed good for fifty years. There never was a Sam Snead before, and there'll never be another one. That's part bragging, but it's also part hard facts. It's impossible, in today's golf, to last. Twenty years is going to be a long time, the maximum anyone is going to be able to play. You've got so many young guys coming out of college today that one's just as good as the next. The long-term guys are going to find it harder and harder to last.

There's also a whole media side to the thing that we didn't have in my day. Certainly nothing like we have now. I got more than my share of headlines and columns when I was starting out, but there was no television in those days, and golf didn't go over so big on the radio.

Freddy Corcoran made sure my name got in the papers. But if I'd had the opportunity to have a press secretary like Arnold Palmer got, and four or five secretaries in the business office and a valet and five lawyers and a business manager, I might have been a folk hero, too. I might have handled it differently, maybe a little better.

Nobody taught me there was money to be made from corporations and magazines until much later. Palmer wasn't born a millionaire, but unlike me, he had advisors who had the benefit of twenty-five years more experience from the growth of the PGA tour. Somebody explained to him, "You sign these autographs and I'll make you a million dollars. You go over here, it'll make you a half a million. You do this today, you do that tomorrow, you make a thirty thousand dollar exhibition over here . . ."

Corcoran and I knew nothing about any of that. We kind of had to invent it as we went along.

Corcoran himself was a fair golfer. We both came on the tour at the same time, in the winter of 1936 over to 1937. He watched me play, and he began to get ideas. Corcoran believed in me. He once said, "No Hollywood script writer could have invented Sam Snead, he was the real article. He had the flavor and tang of authenticity, plus the magic promoters dream about, that extra quality that brings people to the ticket window waving money."

He also once called me "Daniel Boone with a driver."

Fred was a sort of poet. He could talk beautifully about stuff that *might* be there, and which you couldn't prove wasn't there. Take the basic story about me being a hillbilly. That was true, of course. I even preferred to play with my shoes off. I started playing that way when I was a boy and no other way felt natural to me. When we were kids we took our shoes off about the first of May and kept them off until the first frost. Mostly I could anchor myself better by digging in my toes, except on a wet course when you needed cleats. In shoes I felt raised up off the ground, not anchored at all. I once took them off in a national tournament and caught holy hell for it from the other pros. They saw how it was helping me and went off hollering that I wasn't doing things by the book. You can bet they'd've kept their yaps shut if I'd bogeyed a few.

That incident alone wouldn't have changed things

much, except that Fred had a way of getting it into the papers. Fred was very good for the sportswriters. He always had a story about anybody they wanted to know something about. He never had his stories on paper, they were always in his head. Sometimes he let out a secret, and told something kind of private, but then the sportswriters trusted him and would use just about anything he had that day.

My hillbilly background provided golf writers with plenty of grist, and Corcoran kept them well supplied. I don't think I was ever totally the rube they made me out to be, but they loved to hear about how I'd spend time between tours back up at Ashwood with my folks. My roots were up in those hills, and no matter how my career was getting along I found I couldn't stay away from home too long.

I'd get in the car and drive sometimes all night and have breakfast with my mother the next morning. Sometimes I'd come in the door and grab her up and she'd start hollering, "Oh son, watch out, you're gonna hurt my back, you're gonna mess up my hair," or something like that.

So sometimes I'd come in and say, "Hi mom," and go about my business. She'd say "Are you sick? Is something wrong?" She was just being a momma. We got along real well.

I was always doing something that wound up boosting my reputation as a country boy. Stories about me spread in the papers and through the clubhouses. I remember once playing with my nephew J. C. Snead, Ken Dietrich and Chuck Kelly in Boca West. As we came up on the 14th hole, what do you think we saw sitting there

in the middle of the fairway? A cat. I was getting ready
to shoo him away when I took a close look at him and
said, "Jesus, that's a wildcat!"

I'd seen some in the hills when I was growing up. You
could recognize them from the dark spots that run up
their legs. I looked at him and suddenly an urge came
back to me that I hadn't felt since my teen-age years. I
thought, I'm going to try to catch that devil.

Those critters are tough, and they've got four sets of
razors on their paws. But they're only the size of a big
house cat, and I thought that head would look pretty on
my wall. So I took my sweater off, wrapped it around
my hands and tried sneaking up to him. Being down
wind I was able to get pretty close before he decided to
head off for the bushes, but I took a dive for him,
snagged him by the neck and tossed him over my shoulder.

Before he could land on all fours and take off I
whipped around real quick and grabbed his hind legs.
He was really confused by then, and that gave me time
to wrap that sweater around him and jump on him before he had a chance to slash me.

Just then the other guys come driving up in the golf
cart hollering, "What the hell you got there?"

I said, "It's a wildcat!"

They said, "Wha-a?" They couldn't believe it.

I said, "Don't just sit there. Anybody have a big bag
here that's not got anything in the pocket?"

Ken said he did and I told him, "Unzip it and we'll
stuff this thing in there," and I stuffed this wildcat right
down into the big pocket on that golf bag.

After we came in, Chuck says to Mike Manahan,

"Hey Mike, would you bring my jacket out of that white bag?"

When Mike started over to it, I said, "Don't you touch that bag."

He saw then that the damn bag was moving. He jumped back. "What in hell have you got in there, a snake?"

I said, "No, a wildcat."

"You're crazy." He unzipped it a little bit, and those eyes were just sparking and that cat was growling. I realized I was going to have some kind of job getting him out of there.

I sent J. C. down to the hardware store and he came back with a cat collar that I decided to put on the animal for a while. If I could tame him, maybe I could have a pet wildcat.

I put on my gloves and zipped down the bag real carefully. Man, was he mad. I saw he was ready to spring, so I moved my left hand and let him get a good look at that. Meanwhile I sneaked around with my right hand and just as he was ready to spring I grabbed him by the neck and jerked him out of that bag so fast I had him confused again.

J. C. tried to move in and put the collar on him, but he managed to snag J. C. with one claw on his little finger. Ripped it wide open. J. C.'s still got the scar.

I took that cat home and put him on a chain, but during the night he wrapped himself around in it and nearly hung himself. I decided I might as well take him back where I found him and turn him loose. I got my gloves back on and wrestled him into my car, and the first thing he did was slither under the seat and do number two. Holy hell, I had to put all four windows down. I needed a stick to get him out of the car once I got to the golf course, and you should have seen the caddy's eyes bug out when I came up to him with this growling, struggling wildcat and asked him to drive me back out to the green.

I was starting to feel real sorry for this wildcat, so when we finally got there I took out a piece of raw hamburger and put it on the ground as a sort of farewell present. I finally let the cat go, and ROWRRRR, he grabbed that hamburger and socked both claws into it —I guess he thought it was my hand.

I was just standing there watching and I guess the caddy started to get impatient and started complaining. Well, this wildcat looked up and snarled at that caddy. I guess he'd been pretty hungry, all right. But then he went off into the bushes and I guessed that was the end of the wildcat. I handled that critter five or six times and I never even got a scratch.

Fred Corcoran had fun telling that story. One day I asked him to quit it and he said, "It's great for your image, Sam. No golfer in the world has a story to compare to it."

Corcoran was a great guy, a good friend to me. It's true that in the forties, when he had five or six star clients, he was stretched a little thin and it was all he could do trying to handle all them other fellas without going out to beat the bushes for me. But all the same, both of us honored our contract down through the years, even though it was only handwritten on a piece of paper. For my money it might as well have been carved in marble, because he made "Snead" a household name in the history of golf.

WHEN I WAS still hot from the Oakland Open I went down and won $1,000 in the Crosby Tournament, which was big money in those days. We were still in the Depression, and it sure felt good. (You know what they get now for the Crosby? Over a hundred thousand.)

I got used to the money real quick, but never having had much when I was growing up, I wasn't too anxious to part with any. Fred and the other pros saw that I wasn't keen to pull out my money clip so they started to blow up that story right away. Soon I was the guy who was famous for squeezing the nickels till there were buffalo chips coming out of 'em. Fred started to spread tales about my "thriftiness" as they say at St. Andrews, after a little run-in we had at the outset. You see, I had trouble cottoning to this agent stuff. Ten percent! Hell, I was the one out there playing, not him. But eventually I figured ninety percent was better than the none I might get without him running around arranging appearances, especially exhibitions, so I paid up.

In 1938 some of us went up to a fancy Chicago bistro where they had a minimum charge of $3.50 a person. Being raised in the hills, the idea of having to pay money just to sit in a bar sounded like highway robbery. Also, those other guys used to try and play tricks on me and I wasn't sure that this wasn't another one.

All I had all evening was a Coke. Same for my date.

Small wonder I kicked up a fuss when the bill came to seven dollars. That would be a lot for two Cokes even today. You can imagine what it looked like in the Depression.

When the "minimum" part was explained to me, I decided there was no sense in not getting my money's worth. I looked up and down that menu till I found a bottle of wine that just about used up the balance, and I took it home with me.

Not being much of a drinker, that bottle wasn't much use to me personally, so I tried to sell it the next day to one of the other pros I knew to be fond of the grape. Fred Corcoran heard about it, and before you know it every sports columnist in the country was writing about this crazy penny-pinching hick.

That drinking business was kind of a sore point. It's not that I never took a drink in my life. I've had champagne at celebrations and taken a nip here and there at Christmas and such. But there is no way in the world that a man can drink and be an athlete at the same time. Today there's all kinds of scandals going on about cocaine and marijuana and such in the major league sports. The guys who do that are plain fools. To be a winning sportsman you need your body clean and your mind clear. It's a simple fact and there's no getting around it.

The problem back in the thirties was the drink, and some of the players would come onto the course with heads so full of cotton they couldn't see the ball. That was fine with me, because I knew I was going to be the man taking home the potatoes that day. But it didn't make me particularly popular with my fellow pros. I didn't mind, because I had the gallery on my side. I think they followed me because I was so unpredictable. People just seemed to wonder what I was going to do next.

Once during an exhibition match in the South, some smart-aleck marshal goes and announces, "Snead will try to reach the green in two shots." Now who was he to tell me how to lay my shots? I figured I had to show him, so I squared off at that green 300 yards away, swung hard and drove out about twenty yards past the green. Then I hollered out, "I'm sorry, marshal. Will it be all right if I use that second shot to chip back?" The crowd loved that, it was like being a standup comedian. At least I gave the crowd a good laugh.

After Tommy Bolt won the U.S. Open in 1958 he decided for some reason to lace into me, saying that I had an edge around long and blind greens because the fans sometimes helped keep my balls out of the rough. I'm sorry, but I think he was jealous. With that temper of his he could never seem to get the crowds rooting for him. But in a way I don't blame him, or any of the others who took after me.

Out on the course I'd say hello to friends, but that's all. You can't talk to people, or even listen to them, and still hold your concentration. In tournament play every shot counts. One bad shot can lose it all for you.

I've always been a loner. I've always gone my way and let others go theirs. Sometimes I'd rather people just left me alone. Don't get me wrong. I've never outgrown the pleasure of being asked for my autograph. One thing about the public: you've always got to keep yourself in their sights or else they forget about you. Just the same, some of these people will come right out on the course while you're playing. It's enough to drive you nuts. Sometimes kids will come out while you're lining up a shot, and what can you do with everyone watching? You give your ball to them. That's not so bad, but then they'll come out two or three times, and then trade them with their friends, like baseball cards.

Other fan situations aren't bad at all. People will sometimes recognize me by my hat. "I know you," they'll say. That gives you a good feeling, though once somebody said, "Hey there, you're the greatest golfer in the world!"

I said, "Aw, thanks, that's real nice."

But then he called his wife and said, "Hey honey, look, meet *Ben Hogan!*"

Some of the high-living players on the tour resented the fact that I didn't drink while on tour. They thought I should stay up late bending my elbow with them instead of hitting the sack at ten the way I did. They sniped at me, and I guess my being careful with my dough was all they needed to give me a name.

I'd do just enough things to keep the rumor mill turning. I was raised by my momma to do my chores every day. Shining shoes was no big deal and it was good wrist exercise. I took a lot of pride in shining my shoes. I could whip that polishing cloth with the best shoeshine you get on a corner or in a hotel. Cary Middlecoff once walked in on me while I was doing it and I've never heard the end of it from that day to this.

Actually, it was Jimmy Demaret who started maybe the most famous story about me and my money. I once was telling him about how I'd pounded tomato cans into my backyard to use as golf cups, and somehow he turned it around and got the idea that I had money in those cans. Well, the paper had a good chew over that one. People began to say I had millions of dollars buried in tin cans in the West Virginia hills. And you know, just as those revenue agents came after the old moonshiners, they came after me. If any of those cans ever existed, the IRS found every one and emptied them— along with emptying a few I *didn't* have.

But it was too late: my tightness with a buck became a running gag. They'd say, "They never make Sam's pants too long, just the pockets." Whenever my name appeared on a list somewhere, they'd always write my name $am $nead. They said not only did I have the first dollar I ever won, but the interest too. I only wish *that* one were true. There's a hundred variations on it. They said, "Walter Hagen is the first man to make a million dollars at golf and spend it all, but Sam Snead is the first to make a million and save two million."

My answer: most of today's players are millionaires by the time they're thirty, so they don't have the incentive to carry on like I did. Sure, I charged a minimum of $1,000 for exhibitions, plus expenses. But I earned that money. I think it bothered a lot of guys because it looked easy for me. It wasn't.

In my day, hell, the only money I had was what I made at the tournament, and what I could hustle the next day on the tee. In my fifty-year career I earned what was then a record $620,000 in purses up and down both coasts and everywhere in between. That looks sad compared to the pots today.

Most pots in the beginning were no more than five thousand total, with the L.A. Open the richest at ten thousand. Unless you came in first, you didn't carry much home. My first win got me $1,200; the Crosby was $1,000. And you paid your own expenses. In the thirties every poorhouse had its resident golf pro. Guys today are getting forty and fifty thousand for an *exhibition*. Per day. Palmer gets thirty, and I don't think he has won a tournament in nearly fifteen years. His press agents just keep it in front of you what Palmer has done. Good for him.

When I won the British Open in 1946 I got all of $600. It cost me $800 to get over there and back, let alone pay for my caddie and hotel. Wilson sporting goods wanted me to go and they had me under contract. The major money I made over the years wasn't from the matches, it was from those endorsements.

Once I was in Cleveland having a driving contest with Ralph Guldahl. Guldahl, who was signed with Wilson at the time, got up to the tee and wound up putting three balls in the rough. He was so mad he threw down the empty carton that the balls had been in. While I was waiting I just happened to pick up that box, and as I was looking at it some son of a bitch over on the side took a picture. He showed it to the Dunlop man and said, "Snead's playing Wilson balls."

I tried to explain to Dunlop what had happened, but they had that picture of me and wound up offering me only $3,500 to sign again, and I wasn't going for that. Wilson, naturally, liked the picture, and offered me five thousand. Sniffing out the news that I was available, MacGregor then offered me ten, but didn't seem to make it firm. L. B. Icely, another good player of the time, took me aside and offered me some advice. "Son," he said, "I think you can go somewhere with Wilson."

That was a golden steer. I've been with Wilson since 1937—next year it'll be fifty years. I'd say I've made over $3 million with Wilson. It's been very good. They tell me mine was the highest-rated pro name, and they sold more clubs with my name on it than any other, except maybe Nicklaus.

Money and golf will always go together, but it will never be a completely happy marriage. Some amateur golfers would find it a big surprise to learn that golf is about sportsmanship. Most of them think golf is about gambling. Now, I'm not going to say I haven't done my share. I'm going to be talking more about the art of golf hustling later in this book. But you've got to love the game first. If you love gambling first, you're not only going to have no fun golfing, you're probably not going to have a whole lot of luck gambling on it.

The magnitude of this situation didn't dawn on me until I started out on the pro tour. The pots were one source of income, but you could double or triple your winnings the next day when folks from the gallery who thought they were hotshots would call you up and say, "I can offer you a real challenge. And I've got some cash that says it's going to be interesting."

It's one thing to pluck pigeons. It's another thing when

that kind of betting goes on between friends. People think we play for a lot of money, but for a long time we used to play for two dollars. I knew two guys, good buddies for years, and they'd play for four or five hundred dollars a hole and more. They wanted to get me in on it, and I told them they shouldn't play for so goddam much money. Someday one of them was going to cheat, and they'd get so mad they'd lose the friendship.

That doesn't mean that once you decide to bet you don't go at it hammer and tongs. But there's ways to do it right. If you want to bet, you better write those bets down before you start, and make sure it's understood how many shots everybody's getting as a handicap, and what you're playing for.

Did I ever play a bad loser? Every time I play. I never saw a good loser. You show me a good loser and I'll show you a seldom winner. I'm a bad loser myself. I don't want to pay these guys! Even my best friends, we're on the first tee and we make a bet, right away I want to kill them. I have no mercy on them. I grind them right into the green and I expect them to do the same with me. And when I win, I want to be paid on the green. Fast pay keeps the friends.

And friends are mighty important in golf. It being such a lonely game sometimes, you need to have folks you can count on. Even if you're not buddy-buddy, there has to be a certain amount of respect from one player for another.

There was one player I knew, he just died recently, who was okay in many ways but he always wanted to know about anything dirty going on. He was always the one whispering, "Hey, did you know I saw so-and-so coming out of so-and-so's room this morning." Since so many people would tell things about *me* that weren't true, I'd just tell him, "Hell, that don't bother me." He was a gossip, the worst. There are people like that, and you try to stay away from them. If you say anything, they're going to add to it.

Before recently moving to Gleneagles Country Club at Delray Beach, Florida, I lived at the Quail Ridge Club, but I didn't play there for years on account of this guy. After I first joined I was playing there, and a fella by the name of Wally Cessna came up to me and told me there was a club member who was shooting his mouth off about me, saying I was a son of a bitch. I asked Wally to tell me who it was, but he refused. He said, "Just leave it lay, don't mess with it."

Finally, I said, "Wally, is he a friend of yours?"

"Not particularly," he said.

I said, "Am I a friend of yours?"

He said, "Hell, yes!"

And I said, "If somebody was badmouthing you, wouldn't you want to know?"

"All right," Wally said, and he told me his name. He had never even met me.

I called that man right up. I said, "You've been saying some very untruthful things about me and I don't like it. Indians have a word for people like you. You've got a forked tongue."

"Who is this?" he said.

"Sam Snead," I said, and hung up. I wanted to lay into him but I figured it wouldn't do any good.

I'll give you another example. Ralph Guldahl and I used to play a lot of exhibitions together. There was a time when he was the best player in golf. He won the U.S. Open two years running. He beat me out in the Open, beat me out in the Masters and beat me out in the Western—I mean, just by the skin of his teeth, naturally. But, anyway, after these matches I'd have people coming up to me and saying, "That Guldahl is a son of a bitch."

I'd say, "You never met him, how can you say that?"

"That's what I heard."

So I'd say, "Do you go by everything you hear? That Guldahl is one of the most gentle people in the world. Wouldn't say 'boo' to anybody. Tends to his own business, which is more than I can say for some."

Maybe I jumped on them a bit when they said that to me, because there were times when those gossips just nailed me to a cross.

There was a time when I was invited to play at Chuck Kelly's Pine Tree Country Club in Boynton Beach, Florida, which was having its own club championship. I thought it would be fun, as a member, to play in the club championship, but I think I may have showed up too many of the local boys. Pretty soon I got wind that they were cutting me to pieces up there in the locker room. I knew the boys who took care of those lockers, and they told me a certain member had me on the block up there every day, saying, "Who ever heard of an outside pro playing in a club championship?

The next day I was scheduled to play the final against one of my longest-time friends, Ed Tutweiler (who by

the way won the West Virginia Amateur eleven times!).
I knew I had to beat him. And I did—by ten shots. A
week later they had this big dinner for presentation of
the prizes. When they called Tutweiler up, he went on
and on about what a great club they had and all their
great players, and he didn't mention me at all.

When they called my name, I stepped up and said,
"Do you mind if I say something? I never played in a
club championship before. I always wanted to play in
one. But now I'll let out my secret . . . I made it known
to only one man that I wouldn't accept the prize if I won,
and that was Chuck Kelly." Everybody turned right
around and looked at the member who had been badmouthing me, and he was squirming to get under the
table. I went on, "So I'd like to hand this cup to the club
member who scored the lowest, Ed Tutweiler." And I
put that cup in his hands. He was as confused as everyone else, except Chuck and me.

Learning to get along, "to get out of it," and sometimes to swallow your pride is necessary in any sport.
My coming-of-age arrived in the Metropolitan Open at
Forest Hills, New York, in 1937. I'd had a bad run of luck
and needed a win to get me back up on top in the eyes
of the gallery—and in my own, too. Some rain clouds
started to come over, but the weather held long enough
for me to get tied for the lead, having shot a 68 one day,
then 65 the next—the latter a new record for Forest
Hills.

And then it started to rain. And rain. Soon the whole
course was a swamp and some of the pros who hadn't
done too well were saying that the round had to be

discounted. Max Kaesche, chairman of the Metropolitan Golf Association, thought hard about it and finally agreed. Looking at that course, most folks would say he didn't have much of a choice.

Naturally that didn't sit too well with those of us who had been shooting well, and pretty soon Kaesche had a walkout on his hands. It looked like the whole tournament might wind up in the soup. Kaesche came to me. "Sam, are you going to go along with those boys and quit on me?"

I needed that win real bad, and it was just a playoff away. I could taste it. But I told Kaesche, "You did what you thought best, I guess. I'll stay to the finish."

Since I had been tied for first, players farther back than me saw that they had to stay on too. Jimmy Hines and Henry Picard hit a streak then and took that title away from me. Maybe they would have anyway, who knows? But I knew I had done the right thing, and it lifted my name up in a lot of people's eyes. I still talked like a hick, but at least people felt I'd acquired a coating of class. It was one of the only losses in my career where I'd say, "It was worth it."

Fred Corcoran was pretty happy about it, too. The papers at that time were all calling me Slammin' Sam or Slammin' Sammy. To tell the truth, I never liked that nickname much. It implied that I was all power and no finesse. I preferred what one paper called me—"Swingin' Sam." But I know what those other papers were talking about. And they were accurate, for a while. Because I had never taken a golf lesson, my own style of shooting followed what impressed me the most—those power swings . . . ssssWAT! And watching the ball sail. It was the most beautiful part, it earned me my nickname, and to me it will always be the core loveliness of the game of golf. But I came to realize that I needed to do more than slam to keep on making a living.

If you can slam, fine, you've got half the game. But golf is two completely different games: driving and putting. With driving you need strength, and that I had. But in order to putt you have to be a strategist. It's a miniature version of the game and you need to have the stamina, skill and steady hand of a surgeon. My slam was always reliable, and still is. Most of my troubles in the middle of my career were caused by not thinking enough about my putts, about how to plot them.

In fact, I'd put three clubs in the bag as the most important, in this order: the putter, the driver and the wedge. Middlecoff once said, "If you have a good driver, a good putter and a good wedge, you're bodacious." I understand some people now will carry three wedges, but I just carried a sand iron or a pitching wedge and made it do the work of three.

On my putts, I used to talk to the ball. "Go on, baby doll, roll straight over there you pretty little thing. Go on, baby, hop down that little cup. Don't you love your papa?" The sportswriters loved that and so did I. It gave the game some personality. I sincerely believe that it may have helped some putts too. But the truth is, I'd never've needed to sweet talk those balls if I'd worked harder at hitting them right. That's where the concentration of the game came in. And it made all the difference when I took my game into the Seniors.

At age 42 in 1954 at the PGA Championship...

At age 58 in 1970 at the Greenbrier Tournament...

At age 65 in 1977...

And at age 74 in 1986 at The Masters Tournament.

One thing about my slam that not many people knew
. . . I had back troubles that started bad and just kept
getting worse. Those slams began to pain me after a
while, but Fred Corcoran figured there was no sense in
making everybody think I was a cripple.

In fact, I've got the worst-looking back you've ever
seen. I have one more vertebra than the average person.
Dr. Trout, my orthopedic surgeon, once said, "Boy, I'd
swear from looking at your X-rays that you couldn't
play golf or, for that matter, any sport." He couldn't
understand how I got into the service. I can't sit in
one position very long. They wanted to operate, but I
wouldn't have an operation.

There was the time I was one under par going for the
fourth hole. I hit my second shot, and there was an
undulation short of the green that you couldn't see. I
stepped in it and my back went out, and I saw stars. I
pulled up short just off the edge of the green and could
barely chip the ball to the hole. When I got to the next
tee it was so bad I couldn't get the club back, so I quit.
That's happened a number of times, back to when I was
forty-one, the year of the U.S. Open with Hogan the
main competition. I was pretty sure I would have won
it if . . . but who the hell knows?

My back started bothering me during the exhibition.
I think we were playing at Twin Hills in Oklahoma City.
When we came down to Texas it got so bad both my
legs would sort of freeze. During the last round I
couldn't tee my ball up or take it out of the hole. I would
just stop and stand a little bit and it would let go, then
I would walk and it would hit me again. The officials

noticed something was wrong, and I laid it out for them, privately. They wanted to know why in the world I kept on playing and I told them, "I don't want to have to go through all the qualifying rounds again next year."

Which reminds me of something else that started happening around 1936 or 1937, that also became a misery for me. My hair started to fall out! I'd always had straight black hair that was hard as wires, but the Lord must have loved my scalp because starting around then, He—and everybody else—started getting a damned good look at it.

Like my daddy, I didn't like anyone touching my head or fooling with it. As my forehead started to get bigger, the other players started razzing me about it and rubbing it, and there was no way I was going to put up with that. Besides, at tournaments I started getting a little bit distracted, thinking that everybody was looking at my head. I was worried that, instead of watching my golf form, they'd be watching the sun shining off my nude knob.

That put me in mind of the sun beating down on my daddy when he'd tie up those hayshocks back on the farm. He'd wear a big felt hat—not a golf hat, of course, but one of those hats with a big brim to keep the sun off.

Looking around for something like that, I knew I wanted something made of straw that had pores so it could breathe and wouldn't be as hot as a felt hat. I finally found one made by the Dobbs company that felt just right: a snap-brim palmetto. It had this big wide colorful band, which I thought looked kind of snappy, and it sure was easy to spot from way off.

Stories got around about how it was my lucky hat and how I'd had it on the farm. The truth is, as good as that hat was, every time I got stuck in a rainstorm, that was the end of the hat. I'd go through maybe half a dozen to a dozen a year. I liked the design, though, and I stuck to that.

Meanwhile I tried everything to get my hair to grow. I even tried standing on my head, plus every kind of snake oil from here to Timbuktu. A lot of con men walked off with pockets stuffed full of my money, but none of them got a single strand to stand up and take notice. Especially not Tommy Bolt, who once knocked my hat off when there were photographers around. It was a good thing I knew he was kidding or I'd have decked him.

Losing my hair didn't seem to bother the women, though. There were plenty of them around when I started making a name for myself. I had been going with Audrey Karns, dating her since I was in high school. We held hands on the bus and all, real childhood sweethearts, but we kind of got not very far. Then I met this gal down in San Antonio. She was married, but her husband was a drunk, pretty far gone. I thought about marrying her, but my mind was on my game. One night I was out in California and I got a call from her. Her voice sounded funny. Then she told me she had met a doctor and he wanted to marry her. "He's a really nice man, a really nice man," she said. She was trying to get me off the roost, you see. So I said, "Well, if you love him, go ahead." I wasn't ready then, anyway. I was all wrapped up in golf.

It didn't bother me, I just forgot about it. But then my mother died in 1940, and that hit me kind of hard. I'd go home and she wouldn't be there. A big old empty house isn't the kind of place a man wants to come home to. I married my childhood sweetheart Audrey that same year, and we've been married ever since.

PLAYING GOLF IS fun, and learning how to play it in the public eye is one of the most fun things. Doing well is very satisfying, but doing well in front of a crowd— there's nothing like it. I didn't feel the pressure of being what you might call a star. I didn't really know what the hell it was. It used to mean something different than it does today. It was bigger in the sense that you had to do more to get it, but it was also smaller in the sense that the circle of real intense fans was still pretty limited. Still, they'd be taking pictures of you with a pretty girl, and you'd think, Well, jeez, this is pretty good. I enjoyed it.

Of course, publicity cuts two ways. You find that out pretty damned quick when you're up in front of that same crowd and you don't do your best. When you blow up, it's a disaster. The papers get ahold of it and they whoop it up from here to Tuesday. For example, the fact that I never won the U.S. Open has been gone over again and again. Just being in contention is an honor, of course. Being second four times, as I was, is an even greater honor. Once I was tied, only to lose in the playoff. Another time I walked away from the course thinking I'd won, only to have the title slip away two hours later. I'll be talking about those losses in more detail because so much has been said about them —not winning the Open has come down to a golf legend. I'd like to have the last word on it. After all, I'm the one involved. Yes, fame cuts two ways. I'm going to go down in history books not so much for the 165 (135 official) tournaments I've won—including the Masters three times, the PGA national three times and the British Open once—but for the one tournament I never won.

I'll tell you a secret, though. I think the fact I never won the U.S. Open kind of endeared me to golf fans. Some, anyway. They'd come out and root for me, bless them, and my impossible dream in a way became theirs too.

And I'll tell you another secret. The fact that Slammin' Sammy couldn't win the Open made it all the more valuable for the players that did win. Gave it a special quality. I'd say a part of the sheen on that trophy comes from my sweat.

Chapter 5

IT'S NO FUN talking about the U.S. Open. I know they call me the Jinx King: "He never won the U.S. Open." But four times I was runner-up. It's been decades now since I placed in the Open, but sometimes I still twist and turn at night, shooting and reshooting my close calls over and over in my head.

Oh, I've blamed it on the crowd, on the pain in my back and everything else. But thinking about it all these years I've come to the conclusion that my enemy going into the Open was my own publicity. My early wins and the way the papers whooped me up made me too damned cocky. When I first ventured out from The Greenbrier, you'd have thought it was the Second Coming. But when the so-called Jinx started to bite, the laughing was loud and nasty. It's just human nature to want to see the hotshot fall on his face, and, boy, did I ever.

And, boy, did it ever get me down. I know now that the key is to not pay attention to what everybody says but to play your best every day—and play to impress your opponent, not the gallery. But what the hell did I know? I understood the fine points of possums, not of

people. I had me a purple-spotted case of believing-
your-own-publicity.

Now that you've heard me bare my soul—and I'm
going to let you in on what it was like on those greens
—let me leave one small ditty in my corner. I came into
the world of golf at a time when it had the likes of
Guldahl, Demaret, Nelson, Picard, Hogan, Wood, "Lighthorse" Harry Cooper, Walter Hagen, Denny Shute,
Johnny Revolta, Vic Ghezzi, Lloyd Mangrum, Tony
Manero, Paul Runyon, and Lawson Little—to name just
the biggest. Those were some of the greatest golfers
who ever lived. In my first run at the U.S. Open in 1937,
I faced Guldahl, who deserves to be remembered as a
true golf hero. For a couple of years there, Guldahl was
the top of the heap. Nobody, it seemed, could beat him
—including me, as it turned out. Hardly anybody
remembers Ralph now, mostly because his game left
him in the forties, and that was it. He was never able
to make a comeback. It's a shame, but there you are.

At Oakland Hills in Birmingham, Michigan, he was
up against a pretty good field of aces, including Sarazen,
Revolta, Harry Cooper and the reigning champ, Tony
Manero. Now, it's true that none besides Guldahl was
in anything you might call a hot streak (and the bookies
knew it). And it was also true that I came into the Open
as the second-highest moneymaker on the tour that
June. But to give you an idea of the kinds of crazy
"Sneadomania" that was going on, I was the 8-1 odds-
on favorite, even though I'd been in only seven professional tournaments and had won only two of those,

Oakland and the Crosby. Also, I was the first rookie favorite ever.

I don't know what was going on with the bookies, but I can tell you that my standing hadn't gotten me many friends among the pros. And things only got tighter when I scored 136 to qualify and came into the Open with a first-day leading score of 69. My next two rounds weren't as good. I shot an okay 73 and a better 70, which left me tied for second place. Nearly singing out loud, I played the last round for pure joy. I was slamming at the top of my form, 250 yards and more. My irons behaved, shooting truer than William Tell's arrows.

I came to the final hole with 68, and shot an eagle 3 with a three-wood, my spoon and a cute little putt to the cheers of the gallery, making my four-round total 283, very nearly elbowing Manero's record 282 the previous year.

I'd been so full of vinegar that I'd whacked that little joker from tee to green like the devil was after me with a whip. I left the rest of the boys in the dust, and they were still way behind me when I eagled the eighteenth. Figuring nobody was likely to touch my near-record 283, the crowd decided it was all over and nearly carried me back to the clubhouse on their shoulders.

You should have seen the mob of players and fans and reporters and sporting goods people in the locker room, not to mention the ladies trying to sneak in after them. Then and there I was offered contracts to endorse everything from golf equipment to breakfast cereal. Every which way I turned there were these bright eyes and big smiles, and people popping champagne and making toasts. And I felt like King Sam the First.

A couple of former champs were there to relive the glory, too, including 1927 winner Tommy Armour, who told me, "Laddie, you've just won yourself a championship worth more than a seat on the Stock Exchange."

But what neither Tommy nor anybody else knew was that as he was saying that, Ralph Guldahl was still out on the course, coming in slow and steady like the tortoise in the race with the hare. Guldahl was at the height of his Midas touch. He'd done better than expected on the first few holes and needed only to par his way in to equal my 283.

As it turned out, he did even better than that. Eagling one hole, he came in with 281, beating me by two and establishing a new record for the Open that wasn't to be beaten until Hogan's jig in 1948.

Word came in at the back of the crowd, and you'd have thought my end of the locker room was on fire the way it emptied out. A minute before, I was the center of the universe; the next minute I couldn't find a body to give me the time. There's not a feeling in the world like that—like I'd stepped in quicksand and been swallowed up in an instant.

At the time what jagged me the worst was the feeling that I'd had the damned thing in my hands and then had it pulled away. If Guldahl had come back to the clubhouse first, and if I had trailed behind with Bobby Cruickshank, Harry Cooper, Ed Dudley and the others, it wouldn't have been so bad. I was still a kid, just turned twenty-five, and even to come in second in the Open was damned impressive. My time would come.

With all respect to Ralph, who after all was the winner, his way of shooting was old-fashioned, very thought-out and kind of stodgy. The sportswriters were saying I had the most perfect, most natural swing. And soon newcomers were studying my style. Even though I came in second in the Open, offers of money for private lessons swamped The Greenbrier.

But still, it was demoralizing the way I lost. I never went up to the U.S. Open again without thinking, Now don't look the fool like you did in 1937. And every time, that way of thinking beat me before I got to the first tee. If I had won that 1937 title, I believe I'd have knocked over my other three close calls and likely a few more besides.

THAT WINTER I went on what we called the "Grapefruit Circuit." It was a winter tour of opens and tournaments in places like Florida, California, Georgia and North Carolina. Not only were they tropical, but they were pretty juicy too: pros mobbed the events hoping to take home a piece of the $5,000 purses being spread among top scorers at deals like the Los Angeles Open, Greater Greensboro, Oakland and San Francisco.

Not only did I want to dip into that money, I also wanted to prove I was no flash in the pan. In the two weeks after Christmas I earned $2,000 by winning the Miami Open and the Nassau Open and placing fourth in the Miami-Biltmore Open. On top of that I kept my average to under 69 a round for all 12 rounds. I was hot in Miami, scoring a thirteen under par 267.

I stayed hot, winning ten tournaments during the single year of 1938. Those wins included the West Virginia Open and P.G.A. tournaments, the Crosby (for the second year in a row), Chicago, Westchester and the Canadian.

Everywhere I went I got all kinds of press. The other pros couldn't understand why suddenly all the radio guys wanted to interview me. Turns out, my mountain twang went over real well. These guys finally had a golfer who sounded like *something*. For a lot of people in the United States, it was the first time they'd heard any golfer. To them, the voice of golf was my voice.

I did well on the Grapefruit Circuit again in the winter of 1938, and when the new year arrived I decided it was time to try again for the national Open championship, and this time really take that thing home in a sack.

"Spring Mill"—doesn't that name have a pretty sound? Not to me it don't.

That's the name of a club near Philadelphia where the U.S. Open was played in 1939, the same year as the World's Fair and the start of World War II. Actually, the Hitler war seemed about a million miles away and we didn't get involved with it for two more years. Most people were feeling grateful that there were a few more jobs around and that there was finally time to pay attention to having a little fun. People were buying Benny Goodman records, listening to "The Shadow" and "Amos 'n Andy" on the radio.

A few may have turned to the broadcasts of the 1939

U.S. Open coming from Spring Mill. And if they did, they'd have had a chance to hear word of one of the biggest blowups in the history of golf. This blowup was so big, pieces of me were still coming down a week later.

I started off fine with a 68, the best round I'd played all year, which gave me confidence, then a 71, which gave me more. The third round gave me a little trouble. First of all, my back started to bother me. I was feeling all right at the tee but I was worried that one of my slamming swings would pull something. As it turned out, the swing wasn't the problem in that round, it was my putting. One green took me four putts. I closed the third round with a 73.

I was feeling better for the final round. Like in 1937, I roared into the last eighteen full of energy. By the time I had two holes left to play it looked like I had a good chance of breaking 70, which I calculated would put the cup in my pocket. If I parred both holes I'd have a 69 for the last round, a 281 total that would tie Guldahl's 1937 record. It would be a nice way to finish.

I say I "calculated," because that's exactly what I did. With today's computerized scoreboards a player knows where he stands at all times. We had nothing like that back in 1939. We marked our own cards and then doublechecked at the end of each round to make sure the scoring jibed. I knew exactly where I stood, but I had only a fuzzy notion of what the other fellas were doing.

I guessed that the man to beat was Johnny Bulla or Byron Nelson, and I was right about Nelson. He had played on ahead of me, so I didn't have his scores. What I didn't know is that he had finished up with a score of

284, not as good as I thought he would do. If I'd known that was his score, I'd have taken life a little easier on the last two holes. As it was, I was so scared of blowing the Open again I decided to go all out.

I had 272 going into the 17th hole. I smacked a 300-yard drive onto the fairway, but my second shot landed in the rough. I chipped short, had trouble getting the putt in, and wound up with a bogey 5, which made me start sweating, especially when I saw the 550-yard par 5 final hole waiting for me.

I wish I'd known there was no need to sweat. I could have bogeyed that hole too—six shots—and still beaten Nelson's 284. Trouble is, those coming back from the clubhouse knew that fact but, for some reason, decided not to share it with me. They told my partner Ed Dudley, but not me.

Folks got so excited at the prospect of seeing my big comeback win, they began pushing into the fairway. Pressure was so strong, it took the marshals thirty minutes to clear the stretch of ground around that hole. I was stewing every second of it. I wanted to let off a shotgun blast to make those people jump out of my way. I thought about my folks, and about how I'd worked and practiced and prayed to get there, and how big a difference in my bank account a win could make.

And as I'm pacing up and down there waiting for folks to simmer down and clear the green, not one of those folks saw fit to come over and say, "Hold on there, Mr. Snead. Just relax and you'll breeze right into it." Instead I figured I had no more than four more shots, which meant I'd have to birdie the hole if I wanted to avoid a playoff.

When it finally came time to tee up, my teeth were nearly chattering from the tension. It's no wonder that I hooked over into the rough, a section that had been stomped by the crowd. It wasn't serious, but there was still 260 yards to go and not a few bunkers.

It would have made sense for me to play out short with a midiron, then pitch from there. But I still had it in my head that I had to birdie the hole, and had only two strokes left to the cup. Instead of trying to jump back on the fairway and proceeding from there, I took a chance. I decided that my best bet was to aim directly for the flag, and for that I used my trusty two-wood. But I muffed that shot, connecting high on the ball. It looked tired and tumbled toward a sand bunker a little farther down the fairway.

"Giddyap, giddyap, giddyap," I hollered when I saw it losing momentum. And then I commenced squalling "Whoa! Whoa!" when I saw it teetering toward that bunker. In it went. I found it partly buried in fluffy sand, about five feet down from the lip of the trap.

But things weren't hopeless yet. With 100 yards still to go I made a crazy attempt to perform a miracle. Deciding a sand-iron wouldn't make my miracle, I used an eight, which gave the ball lots of power but not much loft. It was exactly the right shot to ram that ball deeply between two chunks of fresh-laid sod at the bunker's lip.

The gallery gave one of those big "Oooooooohhh!" sounds, but I was dumbstruck. This couldn't be happening again, I said to myself. Please, Lord, this can't be happening.

What I really needed then was dynamite, but I settled for trying to explode it out—ball, grass, dirt and everything. I smacked that ball and it flew free for about forty yards before it found another little bunker to snuggle up in.

I figured my chance to win was likely gone, and the best I could do was to get out of the bunker gracefully. Just then, one member of the gallery must have figured I looked like I needed some good news, so he steps over and advises me, "You know, Nelson finished at 284. If you get out in two more, you'll tie him."

If that guy had been close enough, I'd have bent my club around his neck. I was a fool to have taken those chances to get a birdie. . . .

"Why didn't somebody tell me so I could've played it safe?" I hollered. I was spitting. But then I forced myself to cool down, since I still had the slimmest of chances. I got down into a squat and choked up on the club and practically scooped the ball onto the green.

I had one last chance. Everything was now depending on my putt. I have hit 24 holes-in-one in professional tournaments, more than anyone. And I was better at long putts than short ones anyway. I knew that if I made this last shot I'd have a chance against Nelson in the playoff. And then I would not take crazy chances and . . . I made a lot of promises to myself. Then I leaned over and gave that little lady a push.

She rolled so pretty in a slight curve that rolled around the lip of the cup—then scooted past about three feet.

Things got black then. I don't remember seeing a flash

go off, but a picture of me appeared in the papers a few days later, and I looked like a man who'd lost his best friend.

Not giving a damn anymore, I flubbed the three-footer, then finally sent that ball home for a total of 8 strokes. When I leaned over to pull my ball out, that cup looked like the Black Hole of Calcutta. It has haunted me ever since.

To show you how easy that hole was, two other golfers, Shute and Wood, both equaled Nelson's 284, though Nelson beat them in the playoff. My own partner, Ed Dudley, actually birdied that last hole.

That night I was ready to go out with a gun and pay somebody to shoot me. It weighed on my mind so much that I dropped ten pounds, lost more hair and began to choke up even on practice rounds. On top of everything, Guldahl got another piece of my hide by beating me out for the 1939 Masters by a single stroke. My doctor said I was headed for a nervous breakdown.

I spent some time then back at home, and it turned out to be my last summer with my momma before she passed on. Like I said, I got married the next year and things seemed to be going all right even though I finished well back in scores for the 1940 Open and lost the PGA championship to Nelson by one hole in match play. In 1940 I won only three tournaments, my weakest full year of the circuit, but I came back in 1941, winning six tournaments, including the Crosby (for the third time), the Canadian and the North-South.

But the sportswriters didn't get tired of pointing out that after five years on the pro circuit, including thirty-

one Opens, I still didn't have a national title. I was the
"hex-haunted hillbilly," and the jinx theory became established in a lot of people's minds.

IT WASN'T LONG before we all had something more important to think about. After Pearl Harbor, the govern-
ment appropriated The Greenbrier as an internment
center for Japanese and German diplomats during the
months it took to exchange them for our men over there.
With war declared, nobody had to tell us our responsibility was to volunteer for the armed services. My only
decision was over which branch, and I decided on the
navy.

Which, strangely, brings me to what I think must have
been the most thrilling moment of my golf life—the 1942
PGA Championship. And I came this close to not playing in it at all. I'd just passed my physical down at the
navy recruiter, and this brass hat who treated me like
I was his best friend kept pushing his pen at me. "Sign
right here," he said, "and we'll ship the body."

I had the PGA on my mind, so I said, "Whoa, I have
a big golf meet next week. I want one more shot at a title
before I go."

"Oh, we'll give you a pass for that, don't you worry,"
he said. But I had my doubts. "Sign here," he kept saying.

I thought about my wife Audrey, and about the $3,000
purse and $2,000 bonus from Wilson, and I decided the
rest of the boys could handle Tojo all right for just one
more week. Besides, we didn't know if the war would

take a month or a decade. The Nazis had knocked over all of Europe with hardly a peep, and seemed like they might hold out a while.

Little did I realize that my troubles with the armed forces were just starting. I was to play an incredible kid called Jim Turnesa—Corporal Turnesa to Uncle Sam—who was stationed at Fort Dix, New Jersey, not far from the Seaview Country Club in Atlantic City where the championship was being held. Turnesa had beaten both of my rivals, Nelson and Hogan, to face me in the final. To cheer as their buddy was named national PGA champ, 7,000 GIs had been allowed to make the trip from Fort Dix. It was the most hostile gallery I had ever faced. I knew they hated me because they figured I was a lousy civilian. On the other hand, I decided things would get even worse if they knew this was army versus navy, so I didn't let on that I was signing up.

I got my first good look at Turnesa at the first tee. He was a poker-faced little guy, dark-skinned and quiet. Didn't talk nor even move more than seemed absolutely necessary. He was civil, said his hellos and shook hands. But he was there to nail me and went about it as directly as possible. I respected that, and I decided to tip my palmetto to him—after I whipped him.

I hoped to get ahead of him and take the lead advantage, but he played some nice, careful, precise golf and didn't seem fazed by the few bunkers he fell into. Soon he was in front, and his pals were giving me the business every step of the way.

Knowing that I wasn't living up to any fan's expectations actually took a little of the pressure off me. Ed

Dudley, who was acting as marshal for the event, tried to stop the crowd from razzing me and got a little steamed when one of Turnesa's shots in the rough somehow found its way back onto the fairway.

Dudley apologized to me, saying there wasn't much he could do.

"I know it, Ed," I told him. "I ain't complaining."

After twenty-three holes of the thirty-six hole final I was three behind with not much hope of catching up. Still, I remembered how overconfidence had tripped me up in the U.S. Opens, and I tried to play a game that was as quiet and careful as Turnesa's. He was the only quiet thing in the match. Every time I went to putt, those Fort Dix boys would start jabbering and caterwauling. And Dudley kept trying to shut them up.

Finally I said, "Just let them rant and rave, Ed. I'd rather have steady noise than to have it stop for a while and then start again."

"All right," Ed said. He was just doing his job, but being a golfer himself and having had a few noisy galleries of his own, he knew what I was talking about.

Never mind, instead of paying attention to the razz I kept eyeballing Turnesa. The man had a style completely opposite to mine, but I saw that he had a lot of the same pressures on him that I'd had in my two championship blowups. He was being more careful than I'd been; but no matter the cheering he was getting from his boys, I knew the pressure was on him more than on me. He had hauled them all down there on their day's leave, and now he had to give them a show.

Sure enough—on the 24th he slipped, hooking twice

into the rough. I won the hole and that put me within 2 holes of Turnesa and put pressure on him to defend his lead. Instead, I caught up another hole by the 27th, leaving him just 1 ahead and me breathing down his neck.

My championship defeats had left me lean and hard. By that I don't mean my body so much, because I'd always worked out to keep in shape. I meant my morale. Those defeats had toughened me up. The worst had already happened, and there was no place for me to go but up.

That was no skin off Turnesa, though. That little guy didn't shed one bead of sweat. If he was feeling the strain he sure wasn't showing it. He parred the 28th, but I birdied it. The match was even.

Well, you would have thought I was a German or a Jap the way those Fort Dix boys started snarling at me. But I was closing in on Turnesa like a hawk on a delight. I never took my eyes off him, and when he stepped up to play the 29th I saw something that made me want to crow.

Now, let me say that most golfers give their club a little shake before they shoot, kind of a way of keeping your wrists oily and relaxed. Sometimes they'll adjust their grip, too, to get the feel of the club and to make sure you have total control over the shot. Well, I could tell from the way Turnesa waggled his club and fidgeted around with his grip that he could feel every one of his army buddies sitting up there on his shoulders.

A hunting dog can smell when his quarry is running scared, and I smelt it right then. I got you now! I thought. Turnesa drove his first shot into the woods, smacked his recovery shot into a tree and just chopped away out there for a while. He finally came in with a 5 and wasn't able to hit another respectable shot in the championship.

Smelling blood, I started humming the "Merry Widow Waltz," one of my victory songs. I was feeling so high, I made one of the best shots of my career—a 20-yard chip right into the 35th cup for a birdie 2—and so won, two up and one to go.

In a way I felt like I'd done my part for the war effort. I knew that once those army boys got themselves some guns, God help any enemy that got in their way.

When they were handing me the trophy for my first national championship, Turnesa swallowed and said, "Sam, you really came scrambling back."

I thanked him and tipped my hat to him. Though I won the PGA again in 1949 and 1951, that first win in 1942 was my biggest, the one I enjoyed the most. It happened just so quick.

It happens like that sometimes in the major tournaments. People have won them who never won anything before. Nobody even knew they were at the tournament and all of a sudden they won.

I've been very fortunate in my career, and that first PGA established a pattern for me. Sometimes when my stock was at its lowest, something would happen like that and it would shoot right up.

There's a postscript to my PGA story. When I went back to the navy recruiter to sign in and report for duty I remembered our conversation of the week before. "I'm curious about something. If I had signed the enlistment paper, would the navy have let me out for that tournament?" I asked him.

With a straight face the man said, "Negative, Snead."

I look at that PGA trophy now, and remember how I came *that close* to missing it.

So I ENLISTED as a seaman, went through indoctrination at Norfolk and then was to be stationed down in Pensacola to train fliers in gunnery.

After they heard about my championship, they kept me at Norfolk, and I was put on special duty, actually *teaching golf* to pilots. It seems the brass decided that golf was just the right kind of exercise for fliers, who needed to concentrate hard for hours, and golf helped with that. They also needed to get their minds off flying —when you play golf, you forget everything else.

But my hunger to *play* golf actually got me in a spot. Teaching was one thing, but I wanted some action. I would put on civilian clothes and run over to the club near the base and play a round. You know who finally turned me in? The club pro, a fuddy-duddy who maybe didn't like me skimming his action.

My captain called me. "Have you been playing over there?"

"Yes, sir. I'd go there in civilian clothes to play."

"You don't play in uniform?"

"That'd be pretty hard to do, sir. You couldn't swing very well."

"Well, cut it out, sailor."

I did.

Even my hunger for golf could take a vacation. One time I got a weekend off and lined up a nice relaxing stay at a hotel in Virginia Beach, which wasn't too far for my wife to travel. Just before I get ready to go I got a call from Johnny Fisher, the national amateur champ. "We want you to come up to Richmond and play in an exhibition," he said.

"Johnny, this is my weekend off, I want to have a little fun—"

"I'll call you back." He must have done some fast phoning and some fast talking because he called me right back. "Snead, it's an order from the captain. I think you better go."

"I'm on my way." Who can figure a captain?

They had a field day up there. Many of the country's best athletes had signed up for service, and they had an exhibition of some of their best from each branch of the service organized into games of softball, track, touch football, boxing. . . . Here truly were some of the greatest athletes in the country, and there weren't two hundred spectators. If you had that event now you'd fill a stadium. As it was, it mostly made a lot of work downtown for the MPs when it was over.

DURING THE WAR, downtown was generally tough on weekends. After all, you had sailors, soldiers and marines all together down there. With each thinking their branch was the best, you knew stuff was going to fly. You didn't dare take your girlfriend or wife downtown at night or they'd have their hands all over her, and there was no way you were going to fight them off. So you just stayed the hell out of there.

For a while I was transferred to San Diego and had a chance to play golf with a plastic surgeon and an orthopedic surgeon, one a captain and the other a commander, and when those two went out they both used two gloves.

We got to telling stories, and the plastic surgeon said he had had a patient who got into one of those downtown fights, and they bit his nose off.

"This guy showed up with his nose in his hand," said the doc. "I got a picture of him."

"Well," I said, "that's terrible."

"Weren't either," said the doc. "I gave him a better nose than he had."

I GOT TO play plenty of golf in the service, though it was a constant snipe hunt for new balls. Industry, after all, had more important things to make during the war, so we had to use what they called "reprocessed" balls—they'd take an old center and put a new cover on it and called it "reprocessed." Those beauties used to roll out of the box lopsided. One time a player named Bach had to weigh his ball; he was winning everything and people were complaining that the ball was big and heavy. They made him go to a *pharmacist* to get it weighed.

I went into the Navy in '42 and came out in '44, and, no question, I was lucky, being able to continue doing what I do best while those other boys were out there giving their lives. I'm very grateful for it.

About the only thing I disliked about the service, and Lord knows it's minor, was night duty when you had to stand watch and guys would come back and you'd have to log them in "without leave," "too late" and all of that red-tape stuff. That wasn't for me. Mostly I got through it thinking about what I'd do when I got out.

And I couldn't wait to get out to defend my title. All the time that I was in the service I carried the memory of that PGA championship. It was like the keepsake from their sweethearts a lot of the boys were carrying. Considering the Dear John letters, it was more permanent, too, something nobody could ever take away from me.

On the other hand, just as I'd started to believe I was the greatest thing in golf when I set out to win the 1937 Open, I'd come to believe I really had a jinx that would keep me not only from the U.S. Open but from any major tournament.

Losing faith in your ability is the worst thing that can happen to anybody. I'd been on top and at the bottom and in both places at once during those years before World War II. I'd come on the tour thinking I had everything, but it wasn't until the 1942 PGA that I had proved I wasn't just a splash. After winning and enlisting, I honestly thought I might never play again. I was sure lucky there.

Winning the 1942 PGA seemed to prove to the world, and to me, that I'd managed to learn something during those years. And as my tour of duty came to an end, I was rubbing my hands. Once I got back on the tour, I felt sure it was going to be Katy-bar-the-door. I felt alive again.

Chapter 6

I CAME OUT of the service as one of the top people in golf. I'd been around long enough so folks didn't think I was a flash in the pan; I'd been tempered by the heat of nearly three dozen professional tournaments. I still had my hillbilly image, but now folks were used to it and seemed well-disposed toward it. And I finally had a national championship under my belt to show I was more than just a hayseed with a slam.

Many of the big tournaments were suspended during the war, but I did manage to win two of those that were held in 1944, and in 1945 I won at Los Angeles and Dallas. In all, I won five of the first six I played after I got out of the service.

The first was in Portland, Oregon, on a course so muddy the puddles would go right over your shoes. But hell, I just wanted to get at it and *play*.

I ONCE FLEW into Pittsburgh at midnight, then drove down to Morgantown, West Virginia, to play at Lakeview Country Club. That's one tough course. The seventh hole they use for skiing in wintertime. I hit eighteen greens in regulation figures. The next day I missed one green—it's 10,000–1 odds that you're going to hit every green in a tournament. I was playing pretty good; I set six course records in a field that included Jackie Burke and Stan Leonard.

I also set the course record at Sea Island, Georgia. I was playing Paul Harney. The low-round record was 66, and I shot 63. When I came to the last hole, a par five, I said to myself, Well, with a two-iron I might be short and with a one-iron I'm going to be maybe twenty feet past the hole. I was playing good, so I hit the one, figuring I'd be better on the green than short of it. Then Harney and I decided we were going to split eagles, betting $500 for each eagle. I had a 20-25 footer and pffft, in it went. I was riding back with Harney and he seemed to have lost his wallet. I think he believes to this day I got that money. Not so, and he still has the $250 I gave him to put in *his* wallet.

EVEN WITH THESE successes, pressure began to build up for me to take a shot at another major title. Much of the pressure came from Wilson, which wanted to boost my name as much as possible so it could boost sales of sporting goods with my name on them. In 1946 Wilson decided I should go for an international title.

Particularly tempting was the fact that the 1946 British Open, one of the oldest golf events in the world, was being played at St. Andrews, which most folks name as *the* oldest in the world and possibly as the spot where they invented the game of golf we play today. It's like Mecca for golfers; every golfer has to go and play there at least once in his lifetime.

I'd been over to England twice before, though not to the Old Course. I'd gone whooping over there in 1937 when I thought I could whip everybody in the world, and finished a respectable but sobering tenth with a 300. I'd also gone over as a member of the Ryder Cup team before the war.

This time Lawson Little and I shared a cramped little train that squealed and banged all the way up from London, through the Grampians and into Scotland. Was this the British Empire going by through the window, including a patch of awful-looking weeds and rocks that abruptly slowed us down? I turned to a fella across the aisle. "You from around here? Can you tell me what they call that? Looks like an old abandoned golf course."

He looked at me like I was a bug. "My good sir," he sniffed, "that is the Royal and Ancient Club of St. Andrews. It is not now, nor will it ever be, abandoned."

Turns out I was talking to a duke somebody, and no amount of apologizing was able to cool him down. He went right to the papers with it, and I'm telling you, you've never seen anything like the scandal sheets they have over in England. Everywhere I went after that, the local scribes were out for blood.

I think the English still looked way down on Americans, even after the way we helped them in the war. With my accent, and my accidental crack about their all-holy golf course, they started jumping all over me. I think part of their snit came from the fact that there hadn't been a British Open at all since 1939, and they didn't want to see the first comeback tournament won by a foreigner. Meantime, I couldn't find a place to stay or a caddy who knew his job. And the food—whew— all beans and porridge and Cornish pasties. I admit, I couldn't wait to finish playing and get out of there.

I did real well, I think, considering . . . but my competition was hot, too. At the end of the third round I was at 215, but so were Johnny Bulla and Dai Rees.

The last round, I figured, would be tight. The day was windy and rainy, and the golf balls were going every which way but where you wanted them to go. Rees just fell apart, shooting a 42 on the front nine. I wasn't doing too great myself. I double-bogeyed the sixth and whaled my club into the rough in frustration. I hit the turn with a 40. But I figured we were all in the same leaky boat, so I played carefully, taking advantage of those giant St. Andrews greens. My strength still was in my driver, not my putter; but with greens that big, a putt took a major stroke. Things were tough, but they were tough for the whole field, and I started to pull ahead, birdieing the 10th, 12th and 14th.

On the 14th, one man in the gallery, a Scotsman with a beard out to here and looking mournful, told me I could make sixes all the way home and still win. I checked this with a New York *Times* reporter who had the latest World War II technology—a walkie-talkie— and he gave me the straight dope that the match wasn't over yet . . . Bobby Locke and Johnny Bulla were still close behind.

I parred the next three holes—but it was at the famous 17th, the "Road Hole," that I did clinch it. There are a dozen ways to blow that hole, but the wind helped me sink a 25-foot birdie putt, and the title was mine.

Yes, I won, but the experience of "Old Blighty" was enough of a put-off (including the top prize of $600) that I never went back to defend my title. I've said it before and I'll say it again—after the U.S., anything else seems like camping out. I'll admit it, I don't quite follow some of our guys today who talk about *The* Open like it was church.

But being a national and now an international winner had its advantages, including attracting some pretty tony playing partners.

Now, I'm coming to something else that makes golf unlike any other sport in the world. I believe golf, not horse racing, is the true sport of kings. It attracts powerful and talented people from all walks of life like no other sport ever has or can. There are no teams as such, and it's a one-on-one sport, so all kinds of special folks get involved. Tending to be pretty easygoing on the course, telling jokes on the way in and such, I found myself attracting some surprising—for me—playing partners.

In the twenty years after the war this country boy, who learned golfing in the Back Creek Mountains with my pals Piggie McGuffin and Horsehair Brinkley, had the honor of playing with nearly every celebrity from

Bob Hope to the Duke of Windsor—see what I mean about "sport of kings?" Golf also, especially since Eisenhower, is the sport of Presidents, and I've found myself teeing it up with Ike, Nixon and Jerry Ford.

ALL THREE OF these men took their golf seriously. I make it my business to know what a man shoots if I'm going to be playing with him, and I can tell you that Eisenhower was the best of the three. John Kennedy could have been the best of them, but he had his back trouble and so never practiced his golf.

Ike was a great guy. He loved to play golf with me and always asked for me. He always told everyone to call him "Ike" in person, but with my time in the service I couldn't help but think of him as the Commander-in-Chief. I just could never bring myself to call him "Ike" in person, no matter how close we got.

We met on a day when he came down to play at The Greenbrier. It was cold and I had on a big overcoat, so not many people recognized me. There was also a mob of spectators and photographers all over the place.

While we were waiting, one of the photographers running around for a camera angle knocked me back into a hedge. That made me mad. I was about to grab him and have him thrown off the grounds when in comes the President. One of his boys with sharp eyes recognized me and told the President, "That's Sam Snead over there."

Eisenhower says, "Where?" The man pointed at me,

and Ike just plowed through them all and came over. "Hello, Sam," he said. "If you get a chance, maybe we could play golf?"

I swallowed my cud. "When do you want to play, sir?"

"Fifteen minutes?"

I went on down to the club and, sure as you're alive, fifteen minutes later Ike was there, ready to go.

Ike never asked for tips, he had his own game. When I was playing with him at Burning Tree up in Washington, he wasn't doing very well. He had those little glasses, and if he turned his head just a little bit he wouldn't be looking out of those glasses, but out the side. I told him, "Mr. President, I think if you turned a little more . . . here, hit another one."

He said, "You know my pro, Ed Dudley?"

I said, "Yes, sir."

"Well, all *he* ever tells me is 'turn, turn, turn, turn!' "

It seemed Ike was losing sleep over the fact that his short backswing was causing him to lose power on his drives. The problem was so obvious I didn't hesitate to give him my advice: "You've got to stick your butt out more, Mr. President."

His bodyguards couldn't believe I'd said that to the President of the United States. I couldn't believe it either, but Ike was too intent on his game to notice.

"I thought it *was* out," he said.

I thought about his problem, and when I next played with him at Greenbrier and he had his doctor with him I said to the doctor, "Why don't you get him some wraparound eyeglasses, so then he can turn as much as he wants to?"

He did and it worked for Ike, and in appreciation he gave me three of his golf balls, autographed by him. I still have those balls, though they've all turned yellow. Except for Ike, I never went in for autographs for myself, though I have pictures of just about everybody famous I ever played with. (I did once ask for an autograph—the comedian Jack Okie's. I was in the Brown Derby one day and there sat the old boy himself. I went over to him and introduced myself and he said, "Set down, buckaroo," and we sat and talked and got along real nice.) When I look at one of those presidential golf balls I also remember that, after the business with the glasses, I started seeing Ike playing golf in—what else? —a palmetto hat with a wide band, just like mine.

NIXON WASN'T THE player Ike was—never scored as low, though he played pretty often. When he was Ike's number two man he couldn't break 100. He was dying to give Ike a game, so I advised him to use his wedge more, until he felt he had greater control over pitches and chips. Soon he was down into the 80s.

I once played with Nixon for two weeks at Greenbrier, and he was good company. Yes, I liked him, and I think he made a hell of a President. If they went through some of the others like they went through him, well . . . it's too bad. He got caught at something petty that he shouldn't have done, but it shouldn't have made people overlook all the good things. So speaks Sam Snead, golfer-politician. But hell, even a golfer has a right to his opinions.

To tell the truth, I caught Nixon once myself. He'd landed in some really bad rough no one could shoot out of unless you had a bazooka. I was watching him from the fairway when he disappeared into the thicket. Hell, I figured he was going to drop another ball, take his loss like anyone else in that situation and play on. But hell no—out comes his ball flyin' high onto the fairway. Then Nixon comes out of the woods looking real pleased with himself. I knew he threw it out, but I didn't say anything. What could I say? He was the President.

When Ike or Nixon would wind up on the green with putts of no more than, say, four feet, you'd give it to them. Ike would say, "Well, I'm sure I could make that." Though you know if he had to putt them, he'd miss maybe half. So would a lot of pros, for that matter.

There was a time Nixon was playing with me and Arthur Hill, chairman of the board of Greyhound. We started off, and Nixon wound up with a two-footer on the first hole.

He said, "That's good, isn't it?"

And Hill said, "Not for my money it isn't. You've got to putt it."

Nixon said, "But Sam usually gives it to me."

Hill said, "For my money you've got to putt it."

Nixon found out the shorties are hard work. Do you know that he missed every one of those short takes? God, he was red and angry. Sort of like Watergate— silly stuff, getting on edge—for what?

*   *   *

I ALSO PLAYED with the King of Sweden several times. One day after a round he asked me to dinner at the castle. But I had something to do that night and I said I couldn't make it.

Well, Christ, I heard about that later from one of his aides. "The king was not pleased about your declining his invitation. Aren't you interested in visiting a castle? What's wrong with you, Sam?"

I told him I had another engagement that I didn't want to break, castle or no castle.

SPEAKING OF ROYALTY, one of my all-time favorites was the Duke of Windsor. He wasn't what you'd call a real good player, but you could see he really loved the game. He could hold his own, playing with other kings and dukes and earls and like that. I never met anybody like him. He always expected to be treated like a king, but he always treated other people exactly the same way. He never swore. He'd go "tch-tch-tch, what a pity."

The first time I played with him was in Miami. At the time he was the Governor General of the Bahamas. He had a ship that he'd use to go from island to island, and the day Fred Corcoran and I came down the duke invited the old captain of that ship to play with us. I'm telling you, that captain would cuss till he was blue. I had him on one side, and on the other I had the duke going "Tch-tch-tch, what a pity." It was an interesting game.

Afterward the duke came up to Corcoran. "Do you think I should give Sam something?" he asked.

And Fred, knowing how much I loved to see a nice big check, said, "Oh, just give him an autographed picture, I'm sure he'll love that."

So he gave it to me and I went to Freddy and said, "Fred, I can't eat this picture."

The Duke of Windsor was very much the gentleman, but he also had a sense of humor. We were playing out at The Greenbrier and I told a joke. The duke started laughing this very British laugh . . . "ho ho ho ho ho." So I told him another one, a little blue. The guy must never have heard anything like it, because he just went to pieces. His arms were wheeling and he was yelling and hollering. He had a man with him who said, "I never heard the duke laugh like that in my life."

The duke didn't expect to pay for anything anywhere. It was the custom for a king, even one who gave up his throne, to have things gratis. And he knew how to live. They understood and accepted this in England, but Americans sometimes failed to catch on. I remember he stayed at The Homestead back in the '40s and was there for several months with his whole entourage. Well, when he went to leave The Homestead, the concierge gave him a bill that must have topped $200,000. The Duke of Windsor just looked at the concierge and said, "I've never been given one of these in my life. I simply wouldn't know what to do with it." And the concierge was so rattled that he turned the bill over to the manager, who just took the bill and tore it up. Hell, what else could he do? The duke was the duke. I doubt he ever paid that bill, but I'm not criticizing . . . if you and I could live that way, we sure as hell would. The duke went on to The Greenbrier that day and stayed there for a long time too.

But if the duke got most everything handed to him, he still worked hard at his golf. He had this problem: His left foot would come up when he hit and he'd send his ball into orbit, with no distance. He just couldn't hit that ball down. To help, I'd say, "Hit that ball under that bush," and that forced him to start keeping his weight on his left foot, and soon he was able to knock the ball down. Afterward he told me that the only way he could keep his ball down was to try subconsciously to hit "under that bush."

I saw him playing once with these two guys and they were beating the stuff out of him. At the end of the round he stood up and said real quietly, "At the end of six months I shall beat both of you for any amount you name."

He went to an old Scottish pro and said, "I'm putting myself in your hands. I'll do anything you want."

The Scotsman says, "Laddie, you shan't hit a ball for two weeks. You practice the stroke, the stroke, the stroke."

So he didn't hit a ball for two weeks, just practiced his swing. Well, at the end of the six months he went back, met those two guys and cleaned up on both of them.

I WAS PART of the American Ryder Cup team, which played the British three times. One year, after we mopped up there, a couple of us went over to France to play *anybody* . . . they were getting up one of these all-star teams to play us.

I met a Frenchman there who was making a big comeback, and he told me that during the war the Germans had captured him and were getting ready to shoot him, so he jumped over a cliff and broke both legs—which saved his life . . . they shot at him as he jumped, and left him for dead. Now he'd exercised and worked himself back into shape and was back in real contention. That's what I call guts.

Ted Kroll, Jim Turnesa and I were playing a practice round and we got to talking about how we'd all started out as caddies, and as we were walking along who do we see but the Duke of Windsor, sitting there on this shooting cane he always carried.

"Hullo, Sam, how've you been?" he says.

I says, "Pretty."

He tells the other guys, "You know, Sam is double-jointed, that's why he plays so well."

He said it with a straight face, too. Later in the round we picked up a maharaja, then King Leopold of Belgium. When we finished, Fred says to one of the sport scribes, "Hey, I have a little ditty for you."

The reporter looks blank.

"We just finished the first match in history where three ex-kings followed four ex-caddies."

Which was the truth.

Now where else would you have a game like that? No other sport. None.

*   *   *

Fred corcoran and I were over in Rome and we were going to have an audience with the Pope. It was during a time in my career when the yips were really getting to me, I couldn't hole a putt to save my soul. So I asked Fred before we went over, "If I bring my putter, do you think he'd bless it?"

Fred said, "Yeah, sure. He'll bless everything you've got."

I was just kidding, but when we arrived at the Vatican we met this American monsignor who recognized my name, and as we're on our way in, what do you think he starts asking tips on? His putting! That got me laughing, which got him confused.

"Pardon?" the monsignor said.

I explained, "Well, I asked Freddy if I could bring my putter, thinking maybe if the Pope blessed it I'd do better on my own putts. But here you are living with him two years, and your putting's still bad. Now I know I haven't got a flat chance."

My audience with the Pope was in Latin, plus Italian, which was all Greek to this country boy. He was real short and they carried him in on a litter, which the monsignor said they did because he couldn't see over those dividers. The Italians with us were having a good time, laughing and chattering and all, but we were sitting there with mud on our faces, not understanding a word he said.

And speaking of short guys, I got a kick out of playing with Mickey Rooney. He was always trying to run the show, and he had so much nervous energy, everything was done quick. He was also pretty wild with his golf clubs.

There was this time we were playing at Woodland Hills in L.A., which, as its name tells you, is very hilly and full of gullies, ditches and sand traps. As soon as he left the first tee Mickey disappeared. He was out there, but he's so short we couldn't see where he was, which was over one hollow and into the next. We hardly saw him from the tee to the green, but sometimes we'd hear his voice coming from over a hill somewhere, shouting, "I'm here, I'm here!" I felt like I had to keep my eye on him lest he drop into a hole. I was always relieved when I saw his head suddenly popping out of a sand trap.

Mickey, to tell the truth, was a run-of-the-mill golfer. Of all the celebrities I've played with, I'd say the late Bill Holden was the best player, although Randolph Scott was the best putter.

I USED TO play in an exhibition show they called Celebrity Golf. Everybody used to come on that . . . the likes of Dean Martin, Jerry Lewis, Bob Hope, Ray Bolger, Mickey Rooney, Harpo Marx, Milton Berle, Johnny Weismuller, Robert Wagner.

Harpo would come with his toupee on, and of course he'd never say a word. One time he shied away from a shot and I told him, "That lie's not too bad," but Harpo just shook his head and wouldn't go near it.

I said, "Hey, you got to play that."

He whistled and rolled his eyes and pointed down, and there was this little sign on the green that said "Under repair."

"Okay," I said, "but you have to drop it over your shoulder."

So he picked it up and turned his back to the green and *threw* it over his shoulder, but not quite onto the green. It left him with a putt a couple of yards long. A gimme putt? He was nodding like crazy, pleased with himself.

"No, that's not good," I said. "That's not even in the leather."

He got this outraged look on his face, pulled out his putter and stuck the head in the hole. Turns out this putter was made of rubber and he could stretch it right out to that ball to show it was one club length from the hole.

"All right, all right," I told him. You didn't tangle with Harpo—a wonderful funny fellow.

But I think Ray Bolger was the funniest man I ever played with. We were always in competition to see who could tell the best story. Perry Como is funny and enjoyable too, though he's a quiet man, *and* a good story-teller. He'd bring his wife along and we'd all have a ball.

Once Jerry Lewis played with us at a very exclusive club. He was very upset with his game . . . topping the ball for a couple of holes in a row. Finally he said, "I'm so damn shook I don't know where I am. Look at this, I can get up before 150,000 people and ad-lib for an hour and a half, but I can't even get this ball off the ground."

Like they say, golf is a humbling game.

Another time I was playing on Long Island, and Gary Cooper came up to me. "Mr. Snead?"

Pretending not to pay any attention, I just kept playing. He walked up again. "Mr. Snead?"

I turned to him and hit him a little shot in the gut. "What do you mean calling me 'Mr. Snead'?"

Of course he had to hit me back, and he didn't pull his punch too much. Just fun and games among us boys, you understand.

A little less than good, however, also happened in Houston, on a hunting trip with Andy Griffith. (I was there for a celebrity golf show.) He was stretched out a few feet away from me and shooting like crazy—bam, bam, bam.

You'd have thought he'd knocked every duck out of the sky for miles around. I turned to him and said, "Andy, you know I don't see no feathers flying."

He said, "Go to hell," and I swallowed a smile.

I also played once with Paulette Goddard, who was going on the Ed Sullivan show with Errol Flynn. All you heard about then was Flynn and the ladies, and Paulette was a little nervous. I had just won the Palm Beach Round Robin, and when I came to the clubhouse she was talking all upset and you'd think something awful was happening to her.

"What's wrong?" I said.

"Oh, I'm going to see Errol Flynn and I didn't bring a comb."

Well, I always carry one to keep the sideburns trim. I gave it to her and she was real grateful. She was a

gorgeous lady, and I was, naturally, pleased to be of
service.

JACKIE GLEASON? Now there was a man involved with his
game. Once he was in a trap and had the skill to chip
out of there right into the hole—he and Hope and
Crosby had been getting lots of practice in these Pro-
Am tournaments. Anyway, he was so excited about his
miracle recovery that he wandered up to the next tee
and forgot where he'd left his cart. You could hear him
all up and down that course shouting, "Where's my
horse? Where's my horse?"

Gleason was a lot of fun to play with, but he was
damn serious from the first hole to the last. Very competitive. One time he and I played Art Wall and the
band leader Fred Waring down in Delaware. Fred Waring carried all woods in his bag and one iron—a four-
iron. He also parred the first three holes.

Gleason said, "Don't worry about a thing. All his
wheels will fall off in just a few minutes, give him time."
A beat, and then he added, "Even the spare." And sure
enough, they did.

That round was the first time I ever saw Art Wall get
mad. He shot into a trap, and when he got to the bottom
he found that someone had come through and stepped
on his ball, mashing it into the sand. All he found was
someone's footprint with just the tip of the ball peeking
out.

Then when Gleason holed the same shot, he really

blew his stack. I never saw him that way in my life. He came out sputtering "goddam" and turned red as a beet.

SOMETIMES I GET a little too intent myself. I was playing in the Western Open out in Los Angeles and Dennis O'Keefe got mad at me. He was serving as marshal for the event, and I'd gotten so absorbed in a couple of my shots that I'd bumped into him.

He complained to one of the other golfers. "This son of a bitch keeps knocking me down and he hasn't said one word to me."

Well, I just don't pay much attention to people during a round. I'm not looking to see who's there and who's not there, I'm trying to keep my mind on what I'm doing. . . . Now comes the last round and I'm working out a very delicate chip shot. Just as I'm lining up, this guy with Dennis, who's been casing the gallery, suddenly whispers to O'Keefe, "Look at the tits on that blonde!"

I confess. My ears perked right up. I looked around and said, "Where? Where?"

And O'Keefe said, "Ah, he heard *that.*"

WHICH REMINDS ME of my favorite Bob Hope/Bing Crosby story. They were playing together, and Bing had a two-foot putt on a green ringed with people. So Bing gets down on his knees to line up his shot. He's looking at it, and looking at it . . . he gets up and moves to a better angle and looks at it some more every which way.

Hope, impatient, said, "Come *on*."

But Bing just kept looking until it got ridiculous. Finally he got up there and sank it.

As Bing was coming back from the hole, shaking his head, Hope said, "What the hell were you doing back there?"

Bing said, "There was a girl sitting there right in my line, and she had no panties on."

I wasn't there, but I like the story—sort of shows another human side of Bing, who by the way was a fine golfer and friend of golf.

ONE DAY I was talking to Ted Williams in the dugout before a Red Sox game. Some of the Sox were kidding me about the soft life of a professional golfer. Williams said, "Now, you use a club with a flat hitting surface and belt a stationary object. What's so hard about that? I have to stand up there with a round bat and hit a ball that's whizzing by too fast for most people to see it."

"Yeah, Ted," I told him, "but you don't have to go up in the stands and play all your foul balls. I do."

I PLAYED WITH Ernest Hemingway, too, and he was like Ben Hogan—completely silent. He was a tough man, really tough, and he played golf very hard. And there was Hoagy Carmichael, not so much of a golfer but a hell of a nice guy.

I tell you, I'd rather be around a sporting crowd ten to one than so-called normal people. I've seen a lot of different celebrities, all of whom were under pressure at the time. I know some people say most of these celebrities in person aren't so much, but from personal experience I can tell you that I never found one who was a jerk among all the people I played with. They were first class, and maybe that's how they got there to start with.

My celebrity matches included Gene Tunney, Jack Dempsey, and Joe Louis. Joe Louis loved to play, but he was a patsy. God, he lost a lot of money. I found it difficult to beat him out of any kind of money. Joe thought he could play a little better than he could. Once I played him in San Diego and shot 62. And he said, "Who could beat you?"

It turned out he had lost $10,000 betting against me in my first few tournaments after I got out of the service.

Never mind, he was one lovable guy.

ON JUNE 21, 1954, I got my face on the cover of *Time* magazine, but I took it with a grain of salt, like getting your name on the front page of a newspaper. It's a sometime thing. Still, I have to admit it gave me a tingle, sort of certified that old Sam Snead was a celebrity, too. For a while, anyway.

In 1938 I had no national titles yet, but I was doing what I wanted and I felt on top of the world.

Showing how local boy makes good, I offer pointers to President Dwight Eisenhower at The Greenbrier. I never could bring myself to call him "Ike." Credit: Gleneagles Country Club.

Playing with Jackie Gleason at Gleneagles. Credit: Gleneagles Country Club.

Learning a different kind of "slammin'" from Joe Louis in 1951. Credit: Acme.

Jack Dempsey appreciating my good right arm. Credit: Photo by Slantis.

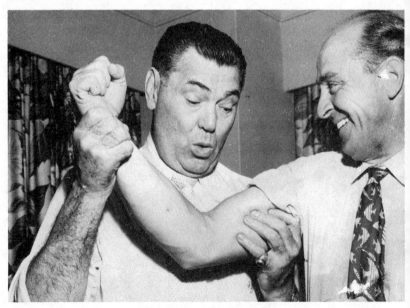

The Duke of Windsor (right) and Chris Dunphy (left) giving me a check for winning The Greenbrier Sam Snead Festival.

The Duke and his Dutchess hobnob with this hillbilly in the early 1950s. (Man at left is unidentified.)

Sharing strategy with Robert McNamara, Secretary of Defense for presidents Kennedy and Johnson. Credit: Greenbrier Club Photos.

At the San Diego Training Center: (left to right) Pat Levinkind, Lou Jenning, Bill Fink, Mrs. Garing, Carol Callender, Babe Didrikson, Sam Snead and Mike Vesock.

Ted Williams took some time off in 1951 to match his angling abilities with mine.

Chapter 7

Yes, for a while ... Somehow I felt like time was going by. Purses were starting to get real healthy, which was fine, but golf was changing from a game to a business. The camaraderie was going; the pros didn't hang around together as much.

Part of this was on account of the motels springing up all over the landscape. ... when the pros would come to town they'd scatter wherever they could find a place. It was and is a blessing to the new pros, what with rooms going for under a hundred dollars a night.

When I started in golf you'd breeze into town and usually there were only one or two places to stay—the club itself or a hotel downtown. All or most of us staying in one place like that, we'd usually get together down in the lobby and there'd be stories told; we were much closer then. Some of the stories became classics, told and retold from one hotel to the next.

I'm including a few here to give an idea of how we lived then, the kinds of things we thought were funny and interesting. They're part of a golfing world that just doesn't exist anymore. Here goes, for better or worse . . .

* * *

—JESUS CAME DOWN and picked Himself out a caddy for a round of golf. On the first hole Jesus said, "Son, what do you think I should hit here?"

The caddy said, "I don't know, Sir, I caddied for Jack Nicklaus and he hit a six-iron here."

"Well," Jesus said, "just give Me a seven."

It happened again at the second hole, and continued throughout the round. When they came to the last hole Jesus asked, "Son, what did Jack hit here?"

"He hit a six-iron, Sir."

Sure enough, Jesus said, "I'll use a seven." So he hit it and it went winging into a lake, and Jesus said, "Son, it went into the water."

The caddy replied, "So did Jack's."

Jesus just looked at him, then started to walk out across the water to get the ball.

As the caddy waited there, another golfer came along and said to the caddy, "Who does that guy think he is, Jesus Christ?"

To which the caddy replied, "He *is* Jesus Christ, but He *thinks* He's Jack Nicklaus."

—A MAN ONCE came up to me at The Greenbrier and asked if I'd give him a lesson. So I went right at it. "First take an eight-iron out of your bag—"

"Wait a minute," said the visitor, "how much is this going to cost me?"

"How much are you willing to pay?"

"Two dollars."

"Put that club back in the bag," I told him. "You've already had two dollars worth."

—A PRO GOLFER had been out on the town and met up with a high-spirited girl. In the hours that followed, she came right down his back with both sets of fingernails, and she just peeled him.

When he went home and took his shirt off, his wife said, "Harry, what in the world are those scratches on you?"

Thinking quickly, he said, "I hit the ball out of bounds and I had to go through a barbed wire fence to get it."

Said she, "But you've got scratches on both sides."

"Well," says he, "I had to come back through it, didn't I?"

—ANOTHER GOLFER WAS coming to inspect the rough where his ball had landed. His wife was with him. He came around a corner and saw that his ball had landed in a honeysuckle bush. Now, if you've ever played golf and you've ever put the ball in the honeysuckle, you know you might as well just wave bye-bye to it because there's no way you're ever going to get it out of that tangle.

But this golfer started beating away at the ball and cussing. Finally his wife put her hands over her ears and said, "They ought to expel you from the tour. That's the worst language I have ever heard in my life!"

The golfer stopped a minute, cocked his head at his wife and sweetly said, "Darlin', I wasn't mad. I just don't like honeysuckle."

—MEN, YOU KNOW that when you're healthy, the eye wanders. Take the pro Ted Kroll: there were were a couple of nice women walking by, and Ted just happened to notice them. Ted's wife dug him with her elbow and said, "Now you stop that, Ted."

And he said, "When I married you I gave you my heart and soul—not my eyes."

—HERE'S A FISH STORY.

I caught black marlin in Pinas Bay, south of Panama, then fished for white marlin outside Caracas and hooked a 209-pound blue marlin.

That line went zinging out of the boat, but before you knew it, I froze up the first reel. Quick as I could, I put another reel on, tied a knot and cut the first reel free. Almost immediately I froze that one up, too. We'd been using a 50-pound test line but the only reel left had a 20-pound test on it. We put it on and tied another knot there.

So we've got a 20-pound test line with two old granny knots in the middle and a 209-pound marlin on the end. We pulled him and played him until he was right up next to the boat, but every time we'd get his head up, he'd pull back down again. One time it seemed like he got out there a mile, but I got him back up again.

"Back up quick," I said. We had been pulling straight up on him, but now we were pulling sideways and he didn't like that, so he had to come. It took everything we had, but finally we jerked that boy right into the boat.

I'VE ALSO HAD some fine experiences hunting all around the world.

I was on a safari in Africa with my son. The organizers wanted me to go up into a lake in Kenya but there were Mau-Maus up there who weren't too friendly. Still, the trip was like the movie *Out of Africa*—everywhere we went we found every kind of game imaginable.

I was out to bag a leopard and a lion. We baited for the leopard by putting meat in a tree and tracked it coming in every evening and every morning. Finally deciding the time had come, we went down to that tree when he was up in it. As we got near we saw the leopard leap right down the trunk head-first . . . those babies don't back down. At first we thought it was coming after us, then we heard a noise coming from a nearby gully.

"What's that noise?" I said.

"Baboon," the guide said. "If he shows up, he'll catch it from that leopard."

You never heard such squalling in your life. The leopard got him, and while that leopard was paying attention to dragging off that baboon, we bagged *him.*

We also got a lion. Again we left bait out and sneaked up on him from behind an anthill. Which sounds funny, except those anthills over there can get as big as a room.

We looked out from around it and there was a lion, just lying out there fifty yards from our bait.

I said, "I can take him." I was shooting a 30.06.

The guide said, "You damn well better. If you just wound him you'll have a maneater on your hands."

While we were talking, that lion must have sensed something, because he bolted off into one of the nearby huts.

It scared the wits out of us; nobody wanted to go near it to get him. The guide said, "We can pitch a tent and wait for him to come out."

"You can wait in a damn tent if you want to, I'll be waiting in the jeep with the windows rolled up. I'm not about to be lion bait," I told him.

Bagging him in that hut wouldn't have been sportsmanlike, so I went home without my lion. I did, though, get an elephant, a buffalo, a zebra, a wildebeest and a hartebeest. The elephant I got in Dar Es Salaam in Tanganyika (Tanzania), where they had the real big tuskers. One side weighs ninety pounds and the other one hundred ten, both about six feet high, though one is a little longer. . . . I guess he was right-handed, so to speak, and used that side more and wore it down.

It never got quiet in Africa. Beyond our campsite we could hear hyena out there crunching on bones. And soft and quiet you'd hear an old lion—rowrrrr. He'd sound like he was two miles off, but he was really sitting out there only fifty yards away.

I was ready to come out after I'd shot all this stuff, but the guide and lead hunter told me he wanted me to shoot an old hippo. I told him forget it. I'd had enough.

You can't go on safaris like that anymore. The animals are protected because they've been overhunted. After working with that hunter, I can understand how it happened.

I'VE ALSO BEEN known to hunt around in roughs for golf balls, and sometimes even that can get a little dangerous.

I was in a pond in Florida with my boots and ball-getter, fishing around in the water for balls. I had one foot on dry land, the other in the pond. So I'm looking around in the water and what do I look down to see? There's an alligator *right there,* within two feet of my foot. It wasn't a tremendous alligator, but he eased right up to me with his mouth open. Those things can run like hell, but that day I ran faster.

Those alligators have some bite. There's an alligator gar, a long fish with a snout that's all teeth, rows and rows, one right after another. Their skins are so tough you can't stick a knife in one, except in the gills. And even that doesn't bother an alligator. They'll just pop one of their "gars" and crunch your knife like a peanut.

I have a friend in Punta Gorda, Florida, whom I hunt quail and turkey with at his hunting club. To get into the club building you have to cross a little bridge over something like a moat. It's got fish in it, but it has alligators all around too; you can see them. A club member was fishing in one of these little johnboats and caught himself a nice bass and was reeling him in when a damn alligator swam up behind, gulped that bass, plug and all, and tried coming up into the boat to have this guy for dessert. He got his ass out of there.

The club's cook also had a narrow scrape. He was out there one day feeding the birds while his wife was watching. All of a sudden she said, "Look out, Henry! That alligator's trying to get between you and the building!" The cook weighed three hundred pounds and he barely made it to the steps on time, even though he set his own personal world's record for the sprint.

They finally trapped that 'gator and took him out of there, but it wasn't any time till he was back, so they shot him. "He had to go," was the verdict. "He had it in his head that he was going to get himself a man, and sooner or later he would've."

HERE'S A SELF-SERVING joke I hope won't offend his Holiness—or even Arnie Palmer.

They're having a huge golf tournament in Rome, with a million dollar first prize. The Pope hears about it and calls together his monsignors and asks if anyone is good enough to play and win first prize. The Vatican could use some fixings. But it seems none of the monsignors can play, so the Pope asks, "Who is the best player in the world?"

One of the monsignors says, "Arnold Palmer."

So the Pope says, "Let's get Arnold Palmer. We'll make him an honorary monsignor and he'll play for us."

They do it, and the Pope tells Arnie, "Monsignor Palmer, we want you to win a tournament for us, we need this money very badly."

"Well, I'll try, Father," says Palmer.

The Pope says, "Since you're the best player in the world, it shouldn't be any problem."

After the tournament Palmer comes back, and the Pope says, "Congratulations for winning all this money for us."

Palmer says, "Sorry, Father, but I didn't win."

"You didn't win? But you're supposed to be the greatest player in the world. Who could beat you?"

And Palmer says, "Rabbi Snead."

BACK IN THE forties a lot of the gamblers wore so-called zoot suits: narrow pants, yellow shoes, a white felt hat and a long chain with a knife on the end of it that they'd twirl.

One of them was walking downtown when a smart-ass kid caught sight of him and started razzing him. "How'd you get them good-looking clothes?"

The gambler turns around, looks at the kid, and says, "Just being smart."

"Yeah?" says the kid. "How do you get to be smart?"

"Well, they have these smart pills. You take them and you get smarter."

"How much are those smart pills?"

"I just happen to have four or five here in my coat, they cost a dollar apiece."

"Well, I got a dollar," says the kid. "Give me one." So he took it, and after a minute he said, "I don't feel no different."

"Well, some people are dumber than others," said the guy in the zoot. "It takes more pills for some."

So the kid said, "Give me another one."

"That'll be another dollar." The kid paid and swallowed it and said nothing was happening. "Better give me the other three." So he paid for them and was getting ready to pop them in his mouth when he noticed something and held up the pills. "Wait a minute," he said, "you know, these look like little turds to me."

And the well-dressed fella said, "There, you see? You're getting smarter already!"

I'VE BEEN OUT on the course several times when lightning struck. Once a bolt came down right near where I was standing with my brother Pete. It killed a girl outright. My brother lived, but the electricity melted his zipper and his belt buckle, went down his leg, burning all the hair off, and went through his foot, burning a little black hole in it. He was lame for a long time afterward. Lee Trevino won't play in lightning since he was hit, and neither should anybody else.

MY LOSS TO Byron Nelson in the 1939 U.S. Open—because of confusion resulting from antiquated scorekeeping—was not the only time primitive scorekeeping was a problem for me. One time in Greensboro, on the seventeenth hole it looked like I was going to win, but my ball hit the side of the green and rolled down into a little crick, a parallel water hazard. The PGA rules committee rep was on hand and said, "Drop here." I did. But the head rules man said, "I don't think you made a proper drop." I said, "Well, I dropped it where they told me to drop it. It's the same place Skip Alexander dropped it."

I went on and made a three on the hole, only to be greeted by the club's tournament chief, who came out and put a two-shot penalty on me for an improper drop. It was the first time in my career I ever heard of an administrator overruling the rules committee.

I tried to protest. "Hey, I did exactly what the rules committee told me. I wasn't any closer to the green. I'd gone back to offset that." It was no use.

According to the rules today, if the committee gave me that ruling I don't think it could be overruled. An official could tell the committee they were wrong and next time it wouldn't be that way, but he couldn't change the ruling once it was made.

THESE ARE A few of the stories I used to tell sitting around at the clubhouse. We would go on for hours, one guy trying to top the other, until finally somebody would pipe up and say, "Enough now, time for some *golf*."

Which is more or less what I'll try to stick to from here on in.

Chapter 8

THE PEAK OF my golfing career was the years 1949 and 1950. I was at the top of my form. I knew enough to cover the mistakes I'd made when I was a kid, and I was only beginning to develop the problems with nerves that drove me crazy later.

I won twenty professional tournaments in those two years alone, and that doesn't include the forty-two other tournaments I played in. Sam Jr. had been born in '44, and young Terrance would be coming along in '52, all of which put me on top of the world professionally *and* personally. Winning the British Open had gotten me respect that even the '42 PGA hadn't, though my first PGA will always be the sweetest to me.

With my confidence back, I won the national PGA again in 1949, plus my first Masters championship. It would have been a perfect year if I'd won the U.S. Open, but that honor stayed out of my way again.

Golf Digest some years later sent all touring pros a form asking our opinions about who was the greatest wedge player, sand player, one-iron player, middle iron, driver . . . Doug Ford and most of the others put "Snead" on all of them. The magazine sent it back: "We don't want to know who the greatest player was; we want to

148

know who is the best in each of these categories." They
got the same reply.

In 1974 the PGA voted me "the greatest player in the
history of golf," which was a nice thing to do for an old
man. What they were voting for, I think, was at least
partly my longevity, plus remembering my golden age in
1949–50.

Sportswriters and fellow pros would analyze my
game in detail, which seems kind of funny since my
game was probably the least calculated on the tour.

Anyway, let me try to take you inside one of my
swings and let you know what it feels like.

Your balance is critical. You see some people who
can sway and can time it—and still get off good shots
because they've done it that way for years and years—
but usually the ones with good balance are more consistent.

You don't have to *do* anything. You can stand on one
leg and play golf. You don't have to take your left heel
off the ground or anything like that, but there are a few
fundamentals you do need to go by.

A lot of people say my lower body is not working well
enough. If I used my legs better I could hit further. Well,
there's truth in that. First I anchor my feet. One of the
reasons I like to play barefoot so much is that I feel like
my toes are roots, just digging down and holding that
ground. Once you've got yourself anchored to the
ground, you have leverage. People have credited the
power of my swing to my muscular shoulders and arms,
and it's true that I could squeeze the latex out of the grip
if I wanted to. But that's not where my power comes

from. It comes from being well planted when I swing.

I may glance up at the pin or the fairway to judge my direction. And my caddy lets me know yardage. But once I've got those things in my head, I don't think about them anymore. I sort of feed it into the little computer in my head; I let *that* do all the aiming and judging power and distance for me. I don't give any of it another thought.

I try to get "oily" instead. Oily is the opposite of jerky. You know, if a baseball pitcher has a herky-jerky motion, he won't last long. Oily means a *smooth* motion. It's the feeling that all your bones and muscles are so in sync, any movement you make is going to be smooth and graceful. Your mind will make a million little corrections as you swing, and it'll be happening way too fast for you to worry about. All you need to do consciously is to be the maintenance man, keeping the works good and loose and *oily*.

Sometimes I'll take a moment to give the ball a little pep talk: "Now stay put, you little fooler, this ain't gonna hurt none at all." Or I use crap-shooting talk: "Come on, little Joe, come to papa." It makes me smile and keeps me loose and light.

When I swing back, I don't coil just my arms; I coil my whole body. If those feet are anchored, you'll literally have the whole weight of the golf course below your feet to help push that ball down the fairway. I don't bunch up the muscles in my body, either. You'll find you don't need to. In fact, when you push yourself to the maximum of your strength, you lose control. I like to use about eighty-five percent of my strength. I try to keep it under control and use it carefully and in a directed way.

In my downswing and follow through, I try for a perfect foot-roll—a pivot on the inside of the right foot that shifts my weight from my resting-aiming stance on the left foot to my powerful driving stance on the right. What it does is use all the power of your stance and your connection with the ground.

When I come down on that ball I'm not "hitting" it; my power isn't directed at smacking the ball. What I'm doing is more like *pushing* the ball. For one instant I want my club head to be *part of the ball*. If your mind is doing what it's supposed to be doing, for that one instant your club will be moving at exactly the right speed and direction to get you where you want to go. And if you're pushing that ball, letting your club head become part of that ball, that ball will go to that place.

If you're oily enough, loose and smooth enough, and have let the ground do the work for you, you should carry through in one smooth single motion and end up in a nice relaxed position with the club over your left shoulder. Let the crowd do all the stretching and straining—to see how far your ball went.

That's it, the essence of my so-called sweet swing, and it won me more than $66,000 in the two years 1949 and 1950, which was real money in those days.

I HAD ALL the students I could handle. There was a big-time musician who came down to Miami, begging me to give him a lesson. It seems he wanted to beat the bandleader Ben Bernie and was willing to pay through the nose for it.

"I want the secret. You know it and I'll give you ten thousand for it," he said.

I wouldn't have minded taking that ten off his hands, but I didn't much care for the way he talked to me. "If I had some kind of secret I wouldn't sell it to anybody," I told him. "Not even for a million."

The real point is, why would anyone think there was one special secret? I'm prejudiced, but I believe golf is the hardest of all sports to play. You need so many varieties of swings and stances for so many lies. Nobody else can help you. It takes more out of you and shows more of a man's character. And so, to be honest, what works for one man may well not work for another. . . .

I was hitting practice balls one time and a man comes up to me and says, "Mr. Snead, I'd like to know what shafts and what swing weights you've got on your clubs —how heavy are they? You know, the works."

"Partner," I said, "I don't know what to tell you. I just swings with 'em until they feels good." (I laid on the old accent a bit.)

Nothing was going to stop this man; he kept asking me this, that, and the other thing, trying to pry that magical "secret" out of me, so finally I said to him, "What do you shoot?"

"Ninety, ninety-five, in there," he said.

I said, "Oh hell, go buy yourself a new glove, anything should help." That was sort of mean, I guess, but I can't help being a little resentful with these fellas. I mean, would he go up to, say, a McEnroe or Lendl and say, Make me an instant tennis whiz, or to Larry Bird and demand to be told the *secret* of his jump shot? But golf ... hell, what's there to smacking a little white ball with pimples? Just the way I make my living, is all . . .

Not everyone was like that fella. Another man watching me on the practice tee says to me, "How do you hit that so soft, with a *three*-iron, that it comes down and stops dead?"

It was a good question, I thought. So I asked him how far he was hitting his three.

He said, "Oh, a hundred thirty, forty yards."

So I said, "What's wrong with that? That's your speed. Don't press it, relax with it and you'll get a softer landing."

I was doing a clinic at The Greenbrier and they had these balls all piled up. I started joking with my caddie, pretending I was mad at him. "I put hook balls and slice balls here, and you got them all mixed up. I might get one or the other. I might tell you I'm going to hook, and it won't hook, it'll want to slice." I tried to keep a straight face.

A guy came over who heard me. He had this anxious but hopeful look on his face. "Can I buy a dozen of those hook balls?" he says. And he said *that* with a straight face. He meant it.

Except for one guy, none of the fellas was looking for real help. What they wanted was a shortcut, a magic potion that they could take and—pop—turn into a golf pro. Plainly put, they were lazy, they wanted instant golf the easy way. Forget it. Hell, it's a pro's bread and butter. He develops a whole repertoire of tips and advice about how to hit this or that. A few tips are useful, especially to the new player or the player with a persistent specific problem. But, in general, the cure is a little pill I call Hard Work.

Like anything, you've got to practice, practice, practice. Of course, first you've got to have the ability, and then the desire. Those two must go together. I don't care how much ability you have; if you don't have desire, you got nothing.

The sister of golf pro Chandler Harper, who played in the Virginia State Open, actually was a better player than her two brothers. Problem was, she didn't like golf. Period. So she just quit. And she was a hell of a player. A lot of people are like that. Sometimes you'll be watching somebody on a practice tee and you say to yourself, This guy ought to win every tournament he's in. He hits it so pure. But then he gets on the tee and they ring the bell and give him a scorecard and a pencil and say, "play away," and then—*boing*—rigor mortis sets in.

Magical handicaps are as much an illusion as magical helpers. That U.S. Open "jinx" business is nonsense. Some of it was psychological, as I've said, but I did have a lot of real and practical problems that wound up keeping me from winning more tournaments. If my early, natural introduction to the game helped make my style unique, it also left me with some stubborn problems that took me years to lick.

The first was the easiest to cure. getting good equipment. I've already told how I found the clubs, one by one, that suited me, but there was more to it than that.

The quality of golf balls has improved so much . . . if I could have played a modern ball in the beginning, way back there in the '30s . . . But the same goes for the rest of the Seniors too.

Nowadays I wouldn't let anybody subsidize me unless they had the equipment I liked best.

Golf pro Clayt Heafner and I were playing out in Salt Lake City once, and my ball was bad. It wasn't more than 150 yards to the fairway, but when I hit my ball I just crunched it . . . and it barely made the fairway. I went over to it and it was as flat as a pill. Heafner with his ball—a Dunlop or MacGregor, I think—beat me for twenty dollars.

A little later Wilson improved its ball, and I've used the Wilson Staff since it first came on the market.

Once you've got the right equipment, you've got to get your head on straight. Different people have different mental approaches. Bobby Locke was a fellow who usually had the most even disposition I ever saw on a golf course, and yet he would sit there, and if you pointed your finger or made a move at the wrong moment, he'd be ready to go to the mat. When he was a kid he used to throw a lot of clubs, and break them in the days when they had wooden shafts. His dad said to him, as I heard it, "If I hear of you ever throwing a club again or breaking one in a fit of temper, you are through with golf." That apparently stopped him.

Bob Jones was a hothead, too. As for me, I've broken clubs and thrown clubs. I still throw one now and again. Usually it's the putter, but from one shot to the next I could cool off. Some people can't; they just keep getting hotter and hotter. The thing is, never follow up a bad shot with another bad shot. Like in fighting . . . if a fighter gets the other guy real mad, he'll burn out quick. It's hard, though, if a guy is beating you. You want to hit him over the head, to kill him.

I confess I've had some friction with other players. I was playing with Lloyd Mangrum in Rochester. We'd played as partners before . . . in fact, I knew Lloyd longer than I knew any other pro, but I never really *knew* him. In a way he reminded me of a tugboat gambler—never let his right hand know what his left was doing.

This time he'd been doing some little things that would bother the average player. I just tried to shut it out. We got to the sixth or seventh hole and he had missed a green short. I was on, about 20 feet from the hole. He chipped by me by 12 feet. Now he's standing with his putter and I thought, He's not going to mark it. So I got up to look my putt over. I didn't see him because I had my back to him. Just as I got ready to draw my putter back he stepped across my line and walked over to mark his ball. I had to back up and start all over.

By the next hole, he must have seen that he'd gotten my dander working a little bit. When we came to the ninth hole I teed up pretty close to the marker, five feet or so, and Lloyd comes and stands next to the marker. Coming on full force now, he leans on his club and starts crossing and uncrossing his feet. I started to blow, but then I held onto it, backed off and said, "Lloyd, I'm giving you every opportunity to play your game, and that's all I'm asking from you. Now you get the hell off the tee until I shoot."

The guy we were playing with says, "Attaboy Snead, he's been doing it to ya every hole." Then it got worse. "Hey," he shouted on one of my backswings, "watch that out of bounds."

From then on we played like two icebergs. I'd gotten so far ahead there was nothing left but to rattle me. I channeled my anger into determination. I told myself, "I'm going to make every shot, I'm going to hole every putt."

I call that kind of channeled anger "cool-mad." Winning takes power. Power can come from positive feelings and self-confidence, but the real pro learns how to take every kind of emotion from love to hate and convert them into power. I was mad as hell at Lloyd that day, and I won the match going away.

If you don't channel anger, it can work the other way —you're so mad you just hit at the ball and lose what people call *tempo*. I just call it *timing*. A golf swing is nothing but coordination and timing. A split second, that's all it is. Whether it's going to the right or left or whatever, it's a very fine line. That's why a lot of fellas don't last too long—two, three years, for example. The good ones, the real good ones, will go up and down like the stock market, but they'll always come back up again.

I was very fortunate. I'd have a real good tournament, play two or three weeks real good, then kind of slough off a bit. I wouldn't let it get to me, and sooner or later the touch would come back.

THERE'S ANOTHER IMPORTANT point that a lot of professional players today forget, and it hurts their game:

sometimes you have to put your clubs away and do
something else. Mostly, I golf every day . . . even when
I went on that African safari I made sure to get in
practice, including the time we ran out of golf balls and
I was hitting elephant turds . . . But every now and then
I put those clubs in the closet and I go fishing. Since I
couldn't always get away on remote trips any more, I
stocked my own pond and had a lot of fun . . . until
Hurricane Gloria filled it up so high the dam broke.

Even in my prime, when I was playing tournament
after tournament back to back, I made a rule that when
I came home to do my income tax, I'd take that week
off and rest. You just can't concentrate and keep it going
without a break. You must rest a little bit. It's like somebody trying to be a fighter every week. After a while it'll
get to you. You notice yourself taking shots that make
you wonder, "What the hell was I *thinking* about?"

Golf, as anyone who's ever played it seriously knows,
requires intense concentration—I mean intense, *at the
moment*. I needed shorter rests, too, before and after
tournaments. For a while I tried to bring my wife and
Sam Jr. along, because it could get pretty lonely out
there on the tour. But as much as I liked to have them
along, I'd come in after a not very good round, and
Audrey'd say, "Okay I've had the boy all day, now he's
yours." That could be hard.

Jimmy Thomson's wife, Viola, once said, "When your
husband comes in with cockleberry burrs on his pants
and sand in his cuffs, don't ask him what he shot."

Sometimes I'd wind up taking Sam Jr. to dinners when
I just wanted to lie down and forget about the day.

Being a parent and a golf pro at the same time is a lot of responsibility. Sometimes your game suffers, sometimes your family suffers. Sometimes both. On the other hand, I know guys who'll take three or four kids with them and say, "I just love having them along." I tell them I don't know how they do it, that it would knock me ten ways from Sunday.

When Bob Goalby got to be the chairman of the PGA Senior Tour he would make four or five phone calls every night, and soon all that work and responsibility began to reflect on his golf. He was losing rounds and putting badly, so I said to him, "Bob, is it worth that much? I know it's affecting you, I can see it. They're playing and thinking golf, and you're thinking of something else."

Bob moved from the chairmanship to the policy board, where he doesn't have to worry about so much stuff, and sure enough, he's playing better now.

He's a great guy and real close friend, but there was a time when Bob Goalby was ready to fight at the drop of a hat. Everything bothered him. We were playing together in the PGA at Akron and were coming down to the 16th hole. As I was lining up my shot, a reporter with a camera snapped my picture. I didn't like it very much, but I didn't say anything. Bob, though, went over and got on this guy, who felt he was just doing his job. Pretty soon they started yelling at each other. I went over to them and said, "Bob, what are you doing?"

"This guy was bothering you, I could see it," he said.

"Bob," I said, "I know, but if he's bothering me I'll handle it. I'll tell you something, if I didn't like you, I'd help this guy. You let too many things bother you. You've got to take the bitter with the sweet."

Bob, not feeling too sweet, says, "When did I get anything sweet?"

"Just knuckle down and keep your nose to it," I told him. "Everybody's going to miss shots. You have different lies, different stances, different conditions. You just can't handle all of them. Everyone's going to make a boo-boo here and there. Walter Hagen used to say if he didn't hit any more than seven bad shots in a round he figured he played a hell of a round. Just think about that. We're going to be here three and a half, four hours. You've got to concentrate on every shot, make every one you can. Once it's made, that's it. If you don't realize that, you're going to be back helping your dad train bird dogs."

I did a pretty good job. Goalby went on from there to make a couple of birdies, made the cut, and actually won the next tournament he played. He called me afterward. "Sam, I want to thank you for setting me straight."

That made me feel good.

NEXT TO LOSS of concentration, one of the worst problems is not knowing when to gamble and when to play it safe. Of course it's mostly up to the individual player. If I'd played safe in 1939, I'd have won the Open. In 1950, when I had the low score average, I didn't try to outdrive anybody; I tried to place the ball. Most people think of me as a big driver, but I feel I came into my own as a golfer when I learned to use my irons. I don't care how far you can hit a ball, or how accurate you putt; you don't cut it as a golfer until you are handy with your irons. Woods are for distance, irons for accuracy. Year in, year out, a strong short-iron game will determine how well you'll score. The longer you play golf, the more you'll realize this is gospel.

As for putting, if you concentrate on nothing except how you're going to hit it, you forget about the most important thing—speed. You can even mishit it; but if you have the right speed, you have only one way to sight it—hit the hole dead center.

Often on tight par fives I lay up on my second shot, but actually make some birdies while staying away from those sixes and sevens. If you can save one or two shots every round, look where that will put you on the ladder . . . a couple of strokes can make the difference between first and tenth.

Of course I'm not in favor of playing safe all the time. Get four or five or six under par, then play safe . . . that's not smart. I've found that when you *force* yourself to play safe, you're going to start making a lot of mistakes.

Even as I was enjoying my greatest success in the late 1940s, my biggest challenge began to show its ugly head. It's a condition called the "yips." It's partly psychological, partly physical, and it's got one awful symptom: a fellow's inability to drop short, usually crucial putts . . . because the hand gives a jerk at just the wrong moment.

In my early days it was relatively easy to solve putting problems. Fred Corcoran would tell a story about the tournament where I was scoring in the low 70s for the first three rounds, but then skied to a 76 in the final round.

"We found the trouble," the caddy is supposed to have told Corcoran later.

"Did he correct his swing?" Corcoran asked.

"No, he just shifted his wallet."

Me and my fondness for my money is fair game for jokes, but it was no joke when the yips first showed up during a series of exhibition matches with Bobby Locke in South Africa during 1946–47. They came and went during the next two years, but mostly came.

My velvet swing hasn't left me, but putting has always been my weak spot—from the word go. Early on I'd modeled myself on Bob Jones, letting my wrists guide my stroke. That's fine when you're young and you've got your nerves. But when you get a few years past thirty, "little things" begin to slip, the same little things that help you win golf tournaments.

For the next few years I had a real heartbreaking time of it . . . the greater the pressure, the worse the jab. The shorter the putt, the less the control.

I got a little defensive, realizing that the guys who aren't long hitters, the little guys, do seem to have a finer touch in putting than the power hitters, especially sizeable fellas like me.

So I tried everything—different putters, different grips. But my putts were starting to creep closer to taking up half my score. It's a tribute to my driving and my iron work that I was able to offset it for a while by trimming strokes with those clubs. But sooner or later, I had to fix my putting.

The problem was solved temporarily when I opened my locker at a tournament one day and found a brass center-shaft I'd never used before. I tested it out at the Greater Greensboro Open and sank putts I'd thought were impossible. Because that shaft connects at the middle of the blade instead of at one end, you get hardly any play at the ends of the blade. If you hit dead center of the blade, where the shaft attaches, you know that ball will go where you aim the shaft. That club helped me conquer the yips for the most successful years of my career.

THOUGH I RACKED up three of the major championships —the Masters, the PGA, and the British Open—the U.S. Open, as you know, hung just out of reach. In 1947, ten years after my first disastrous try, I tried again at the St. Louis Country Club in Missouri. Another cliffhanger.

Other players had better starts. Especially Bobby Locke, who had a first round 68 to my 72. But I would be the more consistent player, and by the end of the third round it looked like it was going to be me against Lew "the Chin" Worsham. He played well, I played well. In fact, we played so equally well that at the end of the fourth round we were tied, 282 each, and were forced into a playoff.

We were so closely matched on that playoff that we came up to the 18th hole, our 90th hole together in that tournament, and we were *still* tied.

I never felt more pressure in my career than I did on that hole. On top of everything I was afraid of a yips attack. It was a prime moment for it, I can tell you. The gallery was quiet as a graveyard as we lined up our putts. I was above the hole, facing downhill on a leftward falling slope, which made it a little more difficult than Worsham's uphill-facing lie. I judged my ball to be farthest. And here's where things started to get a little frayed. I glanced at the referee, Ike Grainger, to see if he was ready to signal which of us was away. He didn't move, but I saw that Worsham had his marking coin in his hand. Nobody was saying anything or making any moves, and all eyes seemed to be on me, so I figured it was me who was supposed to putt. I started to line it up.

"What are you doing?" Worsham said.

"I'm putting out."

"Maybe not," he said. "Are you sure you're away? I think maybe I am."

Which of course meant he went first. I was burning up over this delaying tactic as Grainger pulled out his tape measure and confirmed that I was away, by half an inch.

Though I don't think Worsham asked for that measurement on purpose to throw me, it sure had that effect. The pressure plus the delay just bamboozled me. In my mind I decided how I'd run the putt, but my mind changed at the last instant. Not being oily enough, I struck the ball with the wrong speed and amount of borrow for the break. The ball rolled toward the cup, waved hello, and sailed on past about two inches.

Worsham stepped right up then, triumphant, and on that 90th hole managed to drop his putt. He walked away with the U.S. Open championship because of one timely—for him—question, and one plain lousy stroke —all mine.

*   *   *

I WAS STILL determined to win a U.S. Open, but it kept itself out of reach. I came in seven strokes out of first place in 1948, and one stroke behind Cary Middlecoff in 1949. I once figured out that if I'd shot 69 on the final round of all my U.S. Opens, I would have won seven of them. Of course, that kind of "if only" thinking can make you crazy and I don't recommend it. My last real chance was in 1953 against Ben Hogan, the man who was my shadow all my professional life. In many ways the 1953 tournament was the most dramatic U.S. Open I ever played. It was also the most personal.

I'll explain why, but first I'd like you to meet Ben Hogan, known as "the Little Man."

Chapter 9

I'LL SAY THAT Ben Hogan may have been the greatest golfer of my generation. Nobody was as dedicated to golf as he was. He threw everything else aside. We might have been buddies in another life, but it just so happened that we both came into our prime at exactly the same time. It was fated that we'd become the two great rivals of American golf.

Hogan and I played dozens of matches. I can't think of a better example of how hot and heavy our rivalry got than to direct you to the roll of honor at Augusta, where the Masters Tournament is played. For the four years 1951 to 1954, the championship roll reads like this:

1951	Hogan
1952	Snead
1953	Hogan
1954	Snead

That roll also notes that in 1954 we tied at the end of the regulation seventy-two holes, 289-289, and I finally pulled the Green Jacket away from the Little Man in a tie-breaking extra round, 70-71.

Hell yes, we were well matched. Walter Hagen and

Gene Sarazen were rivals during the 1920s, but they didn't go head to head as often, or come so close, as Hogan and I did.

Our rivalry got so intense that it was part of a Hollywood movie, *Follow the Sun*. Well, actually, that was the story of Hogan's life and I appeared in it playing— who else?—myself, as did Jimmy Demaret and Cary Middlecoff playing theirselves. The director might have gotten actors to mimic our words, but they couldn't find anyone who could do a convincing job on our swings. Even the actor playing Hogan couldn't pull off a convincing Hogan swing. They had to make Hogan up to look like the actor who was playing *him* so he could play himself in the action shots.

Follow the Sun opened in March 1951, about the same time that Hogan was returning to my home course of Greenbrier, where he had beaten me the previous year. I think the local Hot Sulphur Springs movie theater struck just the right balance of hospitality and home-team pride when they booked the film that week so Hogan could see it on the marquee as he drove into town. The marquee read:

FOLLOW THE SUN
STARRING SAM SNEAD

Hogan came out of Texas, born just a few months after me. I'm May 1912; Ben's August. He had a tough life. He grew up in a poor family and tried getting on the pro circuit in 1932, but that was about the bottom of the Depression. He worked here and there as an oil rig worker, a mechanic, and at other odd jobs. Like me, he married his childhood sweetheart. Valerie Hogan stood by her husband for richer and for poorer, in sickness and in health.

In the early years it was mostly for poorer. One of my earliest memories of Hogan was him standing outside the Claremont Country Club in Oakland, beating his fists against a brick wall, looking like he was going to bust out in tears. "I can't go another inch," he said. "I'm finished. Some son of a bitch stole the tires off my car." He and Valerie had been struggling around the circuit in a beat-up old jalopy, and it hadn't been the first time he was robbed.

If Hogan had given up then, I might have won a lot more titles. But golf would have been a less interesting sport. We first played each other in San Francisco, but sportswriters didn't start comparing us until after World War Two. We each had our strong and weak points. Hogan was more scientific than me, but I think maybe he spent too much time thinking. I'll say that I had a more natural swing, but I couldn't control it quite as well as Ben could, especially my putting stroke. Hogan had raw power. He could hit a ball nearly as far as I could and still place it accurately. I know he resented that I got better press than he did.

I think Ben thought of me as a prima donna, the favorite of the photographers. Hogan had done a Hollywood screen test once when the pro money wasn't coming in too good, but you couldn't see his features clearly in the news photos they had then. All you could see was his form, which, to tell the truth, didn't photograph as well as mine.

Man, he hated picking up the morning papers and seeing "Snead" everywhere he looked. When Hogan was driving, the gallery watched the fairway to see where and how far it'd go. When I was driving, folks would watch me to see how I was doing it. That comes across in picture after picture. Ben wasn't too happy about that. Soon the other pros knew they could get a rise out of Hogan by bringing up my name and making comparisons—and they sure could do the same with me, by talking up Hogan.

But I always liked playing Hogan. Anybody likes to play a good player. It inspires you to do better yourself. I always thought I was better, though. Or at least just as good. Anybody who doesn't think that shouldn't be out on the course.

On the course, Hogan don't talk at all. I like it that way fine. You feel like, It's just me now. He's not going to say anything that's going to get me to thinking, and I won't say anything to get him thinking. You look down the fairway and you can see the out-of-bounds marker on, say, the right; you don't need some guy saying, "Hey, look out, you're out of bounds on the right." Sometimes when you're thinking about it being there, you make a mistake. The power of suggestion can jump up and bite you.

The most Ben might say was something like, "I think you're away." He went on the principle that he didn't go out there to talk to the gallery or the opponent. He wanted to put all his concentration on what he was doing and wouldn't let any other stuff bother him. I respected that.

Ben was a loner. He wouldn't sign autographs, which didn't win him fans. He'd say "I'll catch you later," and then you wouldn't see him again. So for years I had the gallery on my side in matches with Hogan. It was a big advantage. Hogan was a good player, I was a personality, and sometimes they came just to see me. For the most part Ben took it in stride, although I think he had a real good time when he led me by seven strokes to win the 1948 U.S. Open, his first of four Open wins.

But gallery sympathy switched permanently in 1949. On the way to a tournament on a foggy road in west Texas, the car Ben and Valerie were driving got hit by a big old bus driving in the wrong lane. It was an awful smash-up and, though both of them managed to survive, Ben's legs got all mashed. For a while we all thought he was done for. *Nobody* expected him to play golf again, let alone win tournaments.

But sure enough, in 1950 he announced that he was returning to the circuit, and he was a sentimental favorite when he shot a record twenty-one under par right under my nose at Greenbrier. It was a record I was not able to equal until 1959. That comeback showed such grit, the public's support went completely over to him. He became the sympathetic favorite to win wherever he played—and he won a hell of a lot.

Matters came to a head later in 1950, just eleven months after that bone-crunching crash. The golf world jumped when they heard that Hogan, whose career had looked ended, would now enter the Los Angeles Open.

Everybody knew we were rivals, and they were rooting for the Little Man. That's just human nature. Hogan played with bandages still on his legs, but he played like no invalid I've ever seen.

Ben went out in 34 to tie for an early lead, but he seemed to tire out on the incoming nine and finished with a 73—nothing to be ashamed of for a man who'd practically come back from the grave. I shot 69, and even that left me in fourth place. The star of that day was a hotshot local kid named Jerry Barber, who looked like he might take it away from both of us and who shot a 68.

But Hogan wasn't done yet. The next day he came burning back with a 69. I shot 70, but that Barber kid got another 68. My problem, as it was all during that time, was the yips. My woods and irons were behaving fine, but my putts just wouldn't do what they were supposed to do.

On the third round Barber got *another* 68, but before the rest of the players got in there was a cloudburst and the round was scrubbed, and with it went Barber's third 68. He wasn't able to score that low again.

On the other hand, the day off gave Ben a chance to rest his legs. His amazingly low scores had got him all kinds of press, and the locals were coming out not to cheer the local boy, Barber, but to boo him for giving poor Ben Hogan a hard time.

Not surprising, the kid cracked under the pressure and shot a third-round 72, which was about the end of him. Ben shot another two-under-par 69 and the scribes started warming up their typewriters to report on the greatest comeback in the history of golf.

Meanwhile, everybody had just about forgotten about old Sam Snead. I was wallowing back in fifth place, five behind Barber, ready to bend my putter into a pretzel and scale it out into the Pacific Ocean.

On the final day, Barber fell completely apart with a 79. Hogan shot his third 69 in a row, and the gallery was cheering fit to bust a gut. His final four-round total was 280, four under par, and a damned impressive show.

He finished before I did and marched off to the clubhouse to start giving interviews, just as I had done back at the Oakland Hills clubhouse at my first Open in 1937.

The difference was, in this new script I was cast as the slow and steady Guldahl. I was still out on the course, sizing up the number 12 even as Hogan was popping corks. Folks had good reason to count me out. As it stood then, I needed five birdies in those last seven holes to catch up.

I birdied the 12th and 13th, made par on the 14th, birdied the 15th, parred the 16th, and arrived at the 17th still needing an impossible two more birdies just to tie the hero of the hour.

"Guess I've got to knock a couple in to catch the Little Man," I announced to what was left of the gallery. Nobody laughed, especially when I got my birdie on 17. When I stepped up to the 18th tee, I think a few people were just starting to get that cold suspicion that I was going to be an uncouth rat after all, and take that victory away from Ben Hogan.

Masters Champions: (seated, left to right) Henry Picard, Craig Wood, Horton Smith, Cliff Roberts, Arnold Palmer, Bobby Jones, Sam Snead, Cary Middlecoff, Doug Ford, Herman Kaiser. (Standing, left to right) Jackie Burke, Claude Harmon, Byron Nelson, Ben Hogan, Gene Sarazen. Credit: Morgan Fitz Photographers.

Competing for the International Canada Cup in Japan. Jimmy Demaret is second from the right in front. I'm not sure who that good-looking guy is second from the left in the front row, but he sure has on a great toupee! Fred Corcoran is in the back next to the woman in the flowered kimono.

I'm in heaven over winning the 1951 PGA Championship (my third) against Walter Burkemo. Credit: Acme.

Keeping up the winning form at the Greenbrier in 1952.
Credit: Bill Wasile—Greenbrier.

My arch-rival Ben Hogan (right) and I had our sights set on the same trophy again and again. Here we are practicing in Wentworth, England, preparing for the 1956 International Canada Cup Tournament. We were the U.S. representatives at the tournament, defending the title. Credit: United Press Photo.

Hogan and I in a less competitive moment.

The 18th was a 445 yard par 4, and my approach left me with a 15-foot putt to birdie. The yips, as I've said, seem to hit hardest on short putts, but they left me alone that day—allowed me to sink the putt and catch Hogan. I was proud of that finishing round, even though the people hated me for it. It was a victory of mind over yips, and in some ways was almost as much a triumph for me as it would have been for Hogan. Naturally, the public didn't see it that way.

I was a lot less proud of the playoff round, which was held a week later—not the next day, as they showed in Ben's movie. We were both feeling pretty low, and we played lousy golf. Though I came out on top, in the public's eye it was Hogan who won.

I played ninety-six tournament rounds in 1950 and averaged 69.2, which is still the record. The boys haven't broken that yet. In 1949, the year I won eleven tournaments, Hogan won one. I think I won three times more than anybody else. Still, that one tournament won by Hogan was the U.S. Open, and his fellow pros thought it was such an impressive comeback that they named him golfer of the year. I didn't and don't begrudge him, but that was my best year ever, and if that wasn't good enough to be golfer of the year . . . It would be today, because they go by points, but it was by sentiment then. Besides, I had won golfer of the year in 1949, so maybe they figured that was enough.

Hogan did himself proud again in the 1953 U.S. Open, which was my last serious chance at the cup. The play-by-play didn't do me much credit. The tournament belonged to Ben, 283 to 289. It was his *fourth* U.S. Open

cup, his *third* since he came back from his accident—
an amazing feat in anyone's book.

I won my third PGA Championship in 1951, the same
year Hogan and I started trading the Masters championship back and forth. But whatever else Ben and I had
done in the past, our real cliffhanger came in 1954.

The 1954 Masters wasn't supposed to belong to either
one of us. A wild-shooting amateur named Billy Joe
Patton almost blew the both of us clear out of Georgia.
After leading for two rounds, Patton was five strokes
behind Hogan on the morning of the final. Ben and I
were like Jack Sprat and his missus. I was doing okay
on the fairways but having my usual trouble with the
greens. Hogan was doing fine with his putts but explor-
ing new territory off the tees.

Patton made us both look bad by making birds left
and right—and topping them with a hole-in-one on the
11th, which caught him right up to Hogan, who had been
leading.

When they told Ben, who was back on the 9th, what
was going on up ahead, it seemed to shake him. By the
12th he was so rattled that he hooked into the water and
took a dismal 6.

What he didn't know was that the pressure had gotten to Patton as well. Patton bogeyed the 12th, double-
bogeyed the 13th with a 7, and made a bogey 6 at the
15th. With these two guys doing heavy psychological
damage to each other, I was tiptoeing up behind, playing a straight-ahead par game to tie it up with Ben and
force a playoff.

In the end I took my third Masters by beating the

Little Man 70 to 71 on that playoff round. They don't come any closer than that.

I haven't seen Ben Hogan since he showed up at the Masters in 1980, as I remember it. Byron Nelson did talk to him, and Byron said that Hogan didn't want to come out of his home in the country for anything or anybody. I guess the aftereffects of those awful car crash wounds are a misery to him, and my heart goes out to him.

I entered the Open year after year, and in the '50s *I* was usually picked as a sentimental favorite. But whether it was some kind of jinx or whatever, it seemed that whenever the USGA flag went up at an Open, so did my score. Though I continued to win tourneys right up into the 1970s, the 1954 Masters was my last national title, and I'm proud to have played it with Hogan.

WHILE IN MY heart I knew that U.S. Open cup would never come my way, I secretly harbored one other major goal: I didn't want to hang up my clubs until I'd broken the equivalent of a four-minute mile in golfing and scored a 59. Just under two weeks shy of my forty-seventh birthday I did it—with nine birdies, an eagle, and *only 25 putts.*

It was May 16, 1959, at the Sam Snead Festival held by Greenbrier, that I shot my all-time personal competitive career low of 59, for a four-round total of 259. (Later Al Geiberger would tie that record.) There was a hell of a wind that day, and I came onto the course thinking, I'm going to have me a time licking this baby. I don't remember much of anything except that wind, and how

I was going to play a trick on it if I could. After all, I knew that course well enough . . . I had no business letting down, wind or no wind.

The first hole was a little dogleg to the right. I hit a pretty good drive down the left side, which is the best place to be positioned for your shot into the green. From a downhill lie I walloped it with my trusty eight-iron, keeping it down into the wind, and making sure I didn't overshoot the green. It was a good shot, landing nine feet past the hole, *and* I made the putt. That was a birdie 3.

The second was a straightaway hole, a short 150 yards with the pin in the right-hand corner of the green, which is just beyond a little crick. I played a wind shot, punching a six-iron that stopped eight feet to the right of the hole. I needed two putts for a par 3.

I began the third hole with as near perfect a drive as I ever made, then a real good four-iron into the heavy wind. The ball landed five feet to the left of the hole, a relatively short putt that gave me a worry for a second. I was, frankly, surprised to birdie this 420-yard hole.

On the fourth my drive wound up on the left, leaving the way open for a six-iron shot into the wind that landed four feet to the right of the pin on a green that had two mean sand bunkers cuddled right up to it. I holed that one, too, for a birdie 3.

Another perfect drive on the fifth let me reach for my eight-iron. Ah, but where I'd planned for the ball to stop, bite and spin back, it wandered fifteen feet past the hole. I needed two putts for a par 4.

Feeling like I was on a streak, I hit right at the flag on

number six; but the wind said uh-uh and threw it left, just short of a bunker. I was bold again, pitching at the flag out of the rough. I left myself an 18-foot birdie putt, and I made it.

Trying to fade my drive around the slight number seven dogleg, I landed in the rough. I escaped okay onto the green, but needed two putts for a par 4.

On the eighth I hit my tee shot right out across the pine trees in the corner of the dogleg and ended in perfect position. I hit a nine-iron, and it skipped twelve feet past. I two-putted for a par 4.

I felt I could have done even better on seven and eight, so I went for the pin again on the ninth. I would have been on the green, except my ball hit a woman standing a little too close to the green and it dropped off to the left.

She was okay, and so was I, chipping down and two-putting from 13 feet. This gave me a 31 going out; but since the second nine is considerably tougher, I wasn't even starting to think about a 59, which meant a *28* on the home and more difficult nine.

On the tenth I hit a real good three-wood that landed at the back of the green, but rolled out onto the back collar. I chipped from about a foot and a half away, and made the putt for par 3.

Once again I tried for the flag on the eleventh, and once again got in trouble, rolling the ball into a drainage ditch, where I did get a free lift. My three iron got me back onto the green, and two putts got me into the cup for a par.

It was on the twelfth that I began to realize something

wonderful. I could feel in my gut that the yips had, for once, decided to leave me be. It was a high feeling, a confident feeling. I knew that if I could just drive as good as I knew I could, the putts would take care of themselves. I then began making what I considered the best run of putting in my career, finishing seven under par on the last seven holes.

The twelfth was a perfect drive, followed by a nine iron onto a green you can't see too well from the fairway. I one-putted for a birdy.

On the thirteenth, 400 yards, I hit my drive just perfect, about 145 yards from the green. The green is punch bowl-shaped, and I hit a seven-iron into it that stopped about five feet past the hole. Without the yips, I tapped that putt right into the cup.

The fourteenth I played going into the wind but slightly downhill. I hit a real good five-iron right at the flag and it ended up about 20 feet short. I just knocked the ball at the hole and it went in for a 2.

I hit a huge drive on the 15th, about 330 yards. With the wind off my right shoulder I hit a five-iron at the green, figuring the wind would take it up to the hole. But it hit a soft spot in the fairway and stopped on the front edge of the green. I stepped up and putted the ball into the hole from 30 feet away for an eagle. This was the first time I began to think I had a chance for a 59. All I needed was two birdies on the last three holes.

At sixteen, the longest at 531 yards, I hit another perfect tee shot that cut across the right corner of the dogleg. Then I hit a one-iron that hopped through the narrow opening, right across the green and over the back edge. I made a good chip coming back but it ran seven feet past the hole. With the putt it came to 4, but that was still a birdie on a par 5.

Whew. On seventeen you either used a four-iron and beat the hell out of the ball, or a three and just let it fly. I used a three and it was probably one of the best iron shots I hit during the whole tournament, maybe the best in my life. I hit it high so it wouldn't run, and it stopped five feet above the hole. I played the putt for a little break but hit it too firm, and it slid out of the corner. I settled for a par on that one and then told the gallery, "Well, I got one more to go."

Eighteen is a tough finishing hole—444 yards, par 4. The average player needs a two-wood for his second shot. The tee markers were so far back that I had to tell the crowd to move back and give me swinging room. That put me in mind of when I was back on the farm in Ashford—when I relaxed, let my mind wander back over all the good shots I'd ever made . . . and before I knew it I had just knocked the hell out of that ball. On this hole I had a five-iron left to the green. It was going to be a 59, 60 or 61 shot. I dropped it just to the right of the hole and it jumped forward maybe two or three feet. I had a two-foot putt left. It was a rough little devil with a real quick break to the right. I played it to the outside of the hole. It just caught the lower corner and fell in. Then I did something I'd wanted to do all my life: I marked down the numerals 5 and 9 and the biggest cheer you—anyway, I—ever heard went up from the crowd.

I followed it up the next day with a 63 on my fourth round, equaling Ben Hogan's record 259.

This was my 103rd tournament win—mighty satisfying. I had promised myself that if I ever broke 60, I'd hang up my clubs.

That was one promise I'm glad I broke.

Chapter 10

THE YEAR 1986 was a great one for older golfers: Nicklaus at forty-six winning the Masters, Raymond Floyd at forty-three winning the U.S. Open.

In a way I feel I deserve a share of the credit. Those guys look young next to me, and they must figure that if old Snead is still socking them at his age (I turned seventy-four in May 1986), they've got no excuse to quit.

When I say "socking them," I mean socking them and winning. I finished 1985 with $23,490 in winnings on the PGA Senior Tour. I played in thirteen tournaments and won money in all of them. In the Legends of Golf Tournament in Austin, Texas, I tied for second. Like the title of my 1978 book, Floyd and Nicklaus are really proving that golf begins at forty.

Since turning sixty I have shot my age every year. I'm still hitting my age every week. I don't know how much longer that's going to be good enough, what with the strong new crop of players coming up into the Seniors. Gary Player, for example, is coming in this year, and he's going to be tough to beat. You go into the Seniors at age fifty, so it won't be too long before I'm going to be up against players like Nicklaus, Trevino, and Floyd, too. Heavy stuff.

The Senior Tour is exciting because of the caliber of competition. All the greats are coming on now, and we surely have more top players now than when I first came on in the '60s. Another change that I find personally encouraging is the amount of money showing up. Winners of a tournament can get $40,000, and they prorate it down. That's considerably more than the whole pot we played for in the regular tour when I was a pup. I was the leading money winner in 1938 with $19,534. No wonder everybody wants to play in the Seniors now. They're really starting to roll in off the tour: Chi Chi Rodriguez, Bobby Nichols, Bruce Crampton. In another five or six years they'll have more name players on the Senior Tour than on the regular tour.

On the regular tour, the guys they've got winning . . . you never heard of them, you don't know who they are. If one walked in the door I couldn't tell you who he was. Of course, competition has gotten keener. The key now, more than ever, is who's making the putt. The short game is where the action is.

To show that I'm still looking ahead to my golf future, I recently accepted the post of president of the "Major Champions of Golf," a newly formed group of many of my old friends over 60 years old—including Julie Boros, Doug Ford, Jerry Barber, Art Wall, Ted Kroll, Jack Fleck, and Bob Toski—who have joined together for corporate outings and charity events. It's amazing how popular this group of "senior" Seniors is all over the country.

Playing in the Seniors is by no means all smooth sailing. You get that many old guys together, it can be a lot of egos and midlife crises and such. And there's your own changing game to worry about. If you let it get to you, you'll have trouble. The trick is to treat it like any other challenge.

Some of the players, no matter how good they are, don't like a certain course for a certain reason, or else they don't like the climate . . . it's too hot or too cold or too in-between. It's a considerable problem with older guys. The texture of greens affects a lot of them, but I go along with what Walter Hagen used to say: "You must adjust to the conditions." If you fuss about every little thing that bothers you, you're not going to play. And if you don't play, you'll wind up turning into a piece of furniture in the clubhouse.

One of the guys I use to compete with back in the '30s, he took a pistol and shot himself because he had cancer. So did Hemingway, though he was tough as they come. I don't hold with that kind of thing. Some people, if they're hurting bad enough, sometimes they might want to get right out. But as far as I can see, so long as you've *got* a chance, you've got to *take* a chance.

I remember a time when the sponsors wanted to put up $70,000 for a winner-take-all. One older golfer I know had a chance to get in on it, but decided not to—said he thought he was too old and didn't have a chance. When he told me that, I said, "If I had been there I would have kicked you all the way back to the next country club. You were playing well. You had a *chance.*" But this guy says, "No, I didn't. I felt funny inside knowing I would be playing with much younger guys." I said, "So what? If he had beaten you, so what? How many chances do you get to play one round for $70,000? I would play

Nicklaus and Arnold Palmer for that in a second. Of course, I'm not saying I'd beat both of them. But I'd sure as hell have a shot at it. I'd have that one in a million shot."

Even the likes of a Ben Hogan isn't above getting overwhelmed. I was playing with Hogan in the Kent Cup Matches at Wentworth—they call it Burma Road in England. Hogan was worried about one of the challenging players; he thought the challenger was better than he was. I'd played Hogan's challenger myself a couple of times, so I knew his weaknesses. I told Hogan, "Keep the fire on and that melon will pop right open."

Ben did, and it did, and Hogan won with no problem.

Things may get a little tighter in the Seniors with all these new guys coming aboard, but I'm not all that worried. Even Jack Nicklaus still hasn't topped my official record of eighty-four PGA career wins, and he'll never touch my real total—165, which includes a bunch of regional medals I took home back in the thirties and forties. If he comes up against me in the Seniors he may not get a chance to win another one again. This is no idle boast. I'm prepared to back it up on the course. Then again, I played Nicklaus once and he turned out to be a pretty fair country golfer. I lost the last hole, but on the tenth hole I three-putted, missing a putt that wasn't more than a few inches.

We had gone to the sixteenth hole. My ball went over and down into a bunker at the back of the green, and I heard Nicklaus say, "Watch this, he's not going to be more than three feet from the hole." He was right. It was real close, and I made the putt for the par.

On the last hole he drove into the bunker next to the green, got it out about twenty-five feet from the hole but uphill. I'm on the back of the green, my ball having gone toward the hole and then broken left. He putted from the other direction, and that thing went right into the hole. He beat me right there, birdied the last hole and beat me.

All the same, I bet he won't be against taking a few pieces of advice from me. As a golfer gets older, you'd think he'd have years of wisdom to draw on. Unfortunately, in most cases they have it but they don't use it. It's ego. You have to face the fact that you're not going to play as well as you get older. You're going to lose distance and you're going to lose flexibility. That's God's truth and no way you're going to get around it. However, if you're wise, there are things you can do to turn your age to advantage. Most important of all, there are things you can do to make sure you continue to *enjoy your game*. Nothing is more important than that. You can put that down as Snead's Number One Rule For Aging Golfers.

To be successful in senior golf, *keep the desire to win.* If you put a few dollars on a game when you were younger, keep doing it. Don't pad your handicap, either. Force yourself to play your best and hardest, and play every day. If you'd rather putter than putt, it's all over for you as a golfer.

The smart older golfer knows it's crucial to be patient with himself even when a given round is falling apart. If you have a bad shot or a bad break, you've just got to swallow it and get on to the next hole. No use worrying about what you might have done better. The next shot and the next hole are the only ones you can control. Concentrate on those. If you're busy moaning in your head about how you blew the last hole and thinking, Oh, I must be getting old, you're just done for.

Here's a tip that will work nearly every time. Picture in your mind that your age is a sand bunker or a water hazard. Sometimes you're going to land in one, no matter how hard you try not to. It does no good to yell and gnash your teeth and pitch your clubs around. The only thing that works is figuring out how to get out with as few strokes as possible. Your age is a bunker, and sometimes it will cost you strokes. Don't let worrying about it cost you whole rounds.

Old dogs *can* learn new tricks, but they also need to be careful not to slow down and take shortcuts in practice time. Even though the body may say Whoa, time to slow down and take it easy, an older golfer must maintain a regimen of exercise.

A key to continue winning in the Seniors is not to let yourself get too fat. An overweight golfer, especially an older fella with less flexibility, puts on strokes whenever he puts on pounds. Bobby Jones used to like to take on a few extra pounds before he played in a championship because he felt it gave him something to burn. By the end of the tournament he'd lose all that extra weight plus some more. But Bobby Jones was an unusual man. His kind of metabolism, and self-discipline, is rare.

Most fat players suffer from Fat Man's Slice. They can't make a full backswing with that tire in the way. Without the torso muscles being coiled, it's hard to make a downswing with power. If you have to work your arms around a mountain, you lose your free swing. It cuts your arm speed and slices yards off your drives. I've experienced all this personally, so I know what I'm talking about.

If you've stayed at the table too long all your life and that basketball you're carrying in front looks like it's going to be a permanent part of your equipment, try setting up the ball so you can take as full a backswing as possible, then connect with the ball from inside, along your target line. Hold the club lightly with the fingers of your left hand when you're addressing, and keep that light touch right through the swing. I always favored an easy, slow backswing. Take it even more leisurely if you're overweight, letting your swing overcome the obstacle of your wider girth as it goes along. Also, take a deep breath before you swing; you'll be surprised how much it steadies your nerves. And the width of your stance should be a little wider than your shoulders for good balance; but to get a bead on the target, toe out your left foot toward it.

Practice each step one at a time until all of them become a natural part of your swing. And while you're at it, how about skipping lunch, or at least keeping it to a light bite? Less lunch and more practice tend to make the special stances and tricks unnecessary.

YOUR LEG AND stomach muscles are going to go first. A good fifteen-to-thirty-minute regimen of just stretching will do wonders for you, and you'll feel the results the minute you get out on the course.

The older you get, the more you need a strong torso

that will allow you to keep your swing on the right plane. A good exercise for all players, but especially for older ones, is to buy a weighted club—or weight up an old wood—and just practice swinging. You don't have to be on a golf course; you can do it in your house—just stay away from anything breakable or your wife will kill you. Swing that thing for a few minutes every day and you'll find your swings on the course will improve dramatically. Keep swinging, swinging, swinging that club. If you're doing it right, you'll tone up every muscle from your neck to your ankles.

I'VE LOST AND gained as many as fifteen pounds in a week. I can sure *gain* it now, but I can't lose it. I'm running around 190 or 195, but I should be at 185. I try to get out and play every day, but I find myself sitting in the cart too much. I'm not active enough. I should walk more. The legs begin to get a little weak . . . I saw myself on TV walking up the fairway, and I looked like I was going to fall down. Lord, my legs seemed to be going every which way.

I began to stay away from the cart and walk the course as much as possible. You lose tone in your legs faster than you realize. No matter what anybody tells you, your legs and feet are the most important part of your body for playing golf. A lot of golfers also play tennis; and while tennis is good for your stamina, it's bad for your swing . . . unless you have the concentration to tell your arm muscles, Now this isn't tennis anymore, this is golf, and for golf I want a swing that's all in one plane, down and up, not around and out. Better yet, jog, run in place, skip rope or just take long walks morning and evening. Not only will it improve your game, it will build your stamina and your lung capacity.

I used to get laughs at parties by showing how I could kick my foot up and touch an eight-foot high ceiling or doorway with one foot while the other foot was planted on the ground. I can still do that at seventy-four. It shows the kind of flexibility I've tried to maintain all my adult life.

It's what enabled me, at sixty-two, to place third in the regular PGA national competition one year *after* my nephew, Jesse C. Snead, did the same. I was one of the top fifty money winners that year, and that's not something you do by taking to your rocker and watching golf on TV.

I made myself a promise that I'd get into shape. I'm on a diet now and I'd like to drop fifteen pounds. I was in the hospital last year for the first time . . . had this awful bellyache, and the doctor said I had a gall bladder and pancreas problem. I had so many enzymes going into my bloodstream, he said, that I must have passed a stone coming into the office.

That hospital took blood out of me every day for five days. I couldn't wait to be discharged. Finally I just left. The doctor tried to say he wanted more X-rays, but I told him I'd come back when he was ready to do something. Meanwhile, I was getting out of that place.

He told me I had a bad gall bladder and it was going to have to come out.

I told him, "Not yet."

My biggest worry at this writing is the vision in my right eye, which is practically gone. I've lost depth perception and can't tell how far it is to the pin. A good caddy can help make up the difference. My best caddy by far was Jimmy Steed from Pinehurst. He caddied for me during most of my seven wins at Greensboro and all of my four wins at Pinehurst.

"Let's hit a soft seven," he'd say. Or, "Let's cut a little five, let's draw in a little four." With him it's always been, Let *us* do this, let *us* do that . . . he's like a partner, and he's the one I turned to when my depth perception started to go. We worked as a team. I'd say, "Jimmy, we're not playing by sight anymore, we're playing by yardage." At first he'd bring three or four clubs for me to choose from. "I don't go by yards, I go by sight," he'd say. But we learned together.

I've found that some of my scoring has actually improved! Going by sight, it's hard to tell what the yardage is. A lot of times in front of the green you have hidden ground, and the green looks closer than it actually is. It might be, say, a seven or an eight . . . hard to tell. Now I wish I had gone by yardage back when I started. I'd have won more tournaments, I honestly believe.

Toughest for me is a 30-, 40-, 50-yard shot. It's especially tough chipping a long way off the green. I feel like I hit the shot just right, but then I come up 15, 20 feet short. I'd tell myself I hit it hard enough, but not so. Now I'm trying to play from memory. When my eyes were good I could look at the flag, put my head down, and wouldn't have to look up before I struck the ball. Still, I do pretty good, considering . . .

*   *   *

THAT CENTER-SHAFT PUTTER helped with the yips, but I
started losing confidence in it around 1960.

In the 1966 PGA championship, I developed a jab so
bad that I hit one of my putts twice! After that I started
experimenting with a croquet style for putting. You
straddle the ball with your legs and hold the top of the
club in your left hand and the shaft well down in your
right. It looks like hell, but it's worked for a few golfers
who were either suffering from the same twitching curse
or were just plain bad putters using a conventional
method.

It certainly didn't make me into a great putter, but it
allowed me to make a workable putt. When I used it at
the Masters some years back, Bobby Jones saw me. He
said, "Sam, stop that. That doesn't look like golf."

I told him, "Nobody asks how you looked, just how
you shot."

The PGA didn't like it, though, and made another silly
rule that both feet have to be on the same side of the
ball when you make a stroke. I was determined not to
let them or my twitch put me out of business. I kept the
basics of the stance but positioned the ball to my right.
It took away the advantage of being right behind the
ball and being able to line it up straight on, but it still
made me not need to use my twitchy wrists so much.

I call this putting stance the "sidesaddle." It, too,
looks like hell . . . but it works. I've mastered it to the
point where I'm averaging thirty-three putts a round—
three less than an average of regulation two per hole.
Not so bad.

*   *   *

As YOU GET older you feel changes in your clubs, too. Some that were strong at one time, that you could handle easily, get to feeling a little stiff. My Izett driver that I used from '36 to '70 is on the shelf now. I've been through four drivers since then, adjusting as I get older.

Too many golfers base their choice of clubs on the distances they shot thirty years ago—a big mistake. The ball lands yards short of the target, which adds strokes to their score and makes them feel worse about themselves than they should.

Older golfers especially tend to underclub, and that's ego again. First they refuse to acknowledge that they're going to be losing some yardage as they get older. Then, when a shot falls short, they say, "Well, I'll make up for it on the next shot." Then they wear themselves out trying to sock the pill like Superman when it's just not in them anymore.

That kind of playing just isn't smart. If you keep a realistic attitude about your hitting, club yourself and hit accordingly, you're going to score better, hit shots more accurately and get less worn out.

Some of the younger players jive me about using a five- or six-iron on a shot under a hundred-fifty yards, but I know that that's what I need and they stop laughing when they see me making par. "Know thyself." It'll save your game. My old friends on the tour knew better than to look at my bag to check what club I used on a shot. They never knew *how* I was going to hit . . . firm, soft, high, low, cut, feather, whatever.

Another problem of older golfers, which can get you in a lot of trouble, is forgetfulness. You have to be real careful marking your card because they've gotten very strict about it. I think that's the worst rule in golf. I think if you're cheating, right-on nitty-gritty cheating, that's one thing. But if you're an older fella who plays 72 good holes—all excited about your score and what you're going to get—and you don't check your card too good, that's just a mistake. You shouldn't have to pay for it. But that's not the way it works anymore. If it turns out you had a 5 and you put down a 4, that's it—you go home without a nickel.

Back in my days of the regular tournaments, in my golden age, we used to have to play 36 holes the last day on Sunday. Finally they saw they were missing a day when they could collect admissions, so they expanded it to four days. Bottom line. Usually we only have three rounds, 54 holes, in the Seniors, but we also have to play Thursday and Friday in the pro-ams. Now, sometimes that can be a chore. I mean, you get some people who say, "What's making me *do* that?" *That* being a slice, a hook, who knows? And meanwhile you're trying to concentrate on your own game. Some of the boys get real rude with some of the amateurs, but I found a system that lets me play the way I want and lets the amateurs get their money's worth and go home feeling good. We go to corporate outings and they want you to play three holes with this group, three holes with that group, and three holes with the next. I got around that by saying, "Look, I can make people nervous playing that way. They think, 'This guy is watching me and I'm going to screw up.' And they're self-conscious the whole time I'm with them. How about if I played just one hole with each group? Then they'll pull for me and can putt my ball and we're actually working together on a hole. Everyone has a good time." Instead of playing the same hole over and over, you can go right around, a nice easy 18, and that's it. To tell the truth, I'm beginning to enjoy the one-day corporate outing as much as the three-day tournament. Am I going soft?

On top of everything else, you get a *good* feeling from being older and still being able to whop that ball down the fairway. It's like cheating the hangman. Take Nicklaus now, winning the Masters for the sixth time just when he's getting set to move up into the Seniors. He won't admit it, but I bet one day he'll look back and say that was his greatest win.

I STARTED THIS book by telling you about my family that came before me. Now I've got a family that's coming after me. Of my brothers, Homer and Lyle are dead. But four of us are still living: Jesse, Jenny, Welford and myself. Jess used to play in Hot Springs. My sister never played. Welford was a pro, but he retired a few years ago.

The house I live in now was built on the farm where my dad's dad was born and raised. We have coons and wildcats and deer. Last fall we had this old doe and three fawns and they'd come out and play there right in the field. I've put a salt lick there and throw corn out for them.

I had thirty-three turkeys come around. They feed in

the field, come right in front of the house and preen themselves. Of course if you crack the door, they're gone. But you can look at them out the window and they don't mind. I put out a feed farm for them. We also have grouse and quail on my place all the time, but I never shoot them. Doesn't seem sporting.

Some people go packing in the woods, but hell, we *live* right there so we don't. You could live off these woods, they're so rich. I've forgotten a lot of woodlore now, but it wouldn't take long to sharpen back up if I went back there for a while.

I went home for Christmas last year and was beside myself. It was too *cold,* never got above sixteen. You can't take a tractor or any similar equipment out in the field in such weather . . . they'll go like a sled on the frozen ground. And I have a lot of work to do. The place was flooded during Hurricane Gloria. I had a fish pond almost 200 yards long that I built for the bass and catfish. In comes Gloria, up goes the water level and down goes the dam, taking my lake, my fish and even my boat with it. I thought, Oh God, that boat's gonna wind up down on the golf course, but it never left the premises. We went down to see it two days later and it was as flat as a table. I still get involved in the work on the place. It's as good a golf exercise as any, and it has a practical purpose—which helps keep me from going stir-crazy.

MY SON, SAM JR. (we'd taken to calling him by his nick-name, "Jackie") was supposed to work for me at Green-brier, but he wasn't doing much of anything down there, so I bought the old bank building in Hot Springs and turned it into a tavern and country store. Good name too—"Sam Snead Tavern." Jackie ran that for a while, but we couldn't get a liquor license unless the place could sit fifty-four people. I had to have it redone, which cost me another $110,000. It's a lovely place now. Jackie did the decor. I don't know where he got that from, but he's good at it and has done a fine job running the place.

He's married and has two kids. Cathie, who just turned fifteen, is an outstanding skier. Little Sam, they tell me he's the fastest kid in his grade school. Can he ever run! He's small but tough as a nut. What he lacks in size he makes up for in other ways. Like his granddad, he loves to hunt and fish, and unlike his granddad, he keeps pet snakes. Actually Sam is a better skier than Cathie, but she does the downhill faster. I think you'll hear from both of them one of these days.

EVEN IN HIS seventies, their granddad is still able to make par more often than not. Reasons? Both mental and physical. I was blessed with a strong physique and I keep it in shape as best I can. *And* I still love to play golf, both for fun and competitively.

In the winter I live and play golf at Gleneagles Country Club in Delray Beach, Florida. Stan Abrams of Senior Tour Players, Inc., capitalized on the rising popularity of the Senior Tour and convinced me—along with Billy Casper, Bob Goalby, Doug Sanders, Gay Brewer and Doug Ford—to band together to help promote Gleneagles. I've been told that this combination of golf's "legends" has been quite a success. In the summer I play most of my golf at the Cascades Golf and Tennis Club in Hot Springs, Virginia.

I think the nicest thing ever said about me was said by the Australian pro Peter Thomson: "Like classic plays and symphonies, Sam Snead doesn't just belong to a generation. His mark will be left on golf into eternity."

When folks start saying things like that about you, you figure, well, you must be doing something right.

Chapter 11

WHAT YOU'RE GOING to get here is some this and some that . . . including things I left out up to now when I thought I was done and I was told differently by my collaborator and publisher. Come on, Sam, let's wing it for a while, they said. And that's what I'll do now. If what follows reads like you're sitting around with me at, say, Sleepy Hollow in New York state, you'd be right. That's just what it is, between and after rounds.

Most of my play in the last six years has been with the PGA Senior Tour, created by Fred Raphael and supported by Jimmy Demaret, one of golf's most colorful competitors.

Raphael and Demaret's thinking was that there still seemed to be plenty of interest in the older players. Why not a Seniors tournament? Not match but medal best ball?

I don't know how they settled on the Onion Creek course in Austin, Texas for the first Legends tournament in 1978, but I suspect it was because Jimmy Demaret helped lay that course out.

Like everything else on the tour, play was very informal then. There were no assigned partners. You more or less chose up sides among yourselves and picked

198

whomever you wanted to play with. I paired with Gardner Dickinson and we won that first tournament. It helped that I birdied the last three holes. I was proud to have been on the team that launched the Senior Tour.

It wasn't easy, though. They had us 1-down going into the 16th. Peter Thomson stepped up and holed a 20-footer, and I knew if I didn't make this one we'd be 2-down and two to play. I wanted to avoid that kind of pressure if I could, so I got into the hole right on top of his ball from about 12 feet or so. That got me going, and I holed out at eight feet on the next hole to win that one. Now we were even, now things got hot. I pitched my third shot from down in a blind area; it stopped less than two feet from the hole and I made that to win the match for us, 1-up.

I didn't do as well in the second tournament. The playoff in this one involved Art Wall and Tommy Bolt against Roberto DeVicenzo and Julius Boros.

You've heard a lot about "Terrible-tempered" Tommy Bolt. But Tommy's all right. He goes off a little bit and throws a tantrum now and then but he doesn't mean it. Tommy and I played in The Legends and he was always very nice to me, we got along just fine. At that second Legends tournament he was burning things up. At the first sudden death hole, Tommy holed a 25-footer and shook his finger at DeVicenzo. "Aha, I hung your ass with that one!"

DeVicenzo rolled in one from almost the same distance right on top of it, and then it was his turn to shake his finger back at Tommy. They went six straight holes in birdies. It brought the people right up off their seats cheering, like they were at the Super Bowl or something.

Part of the Legends' success, of course, came from the fact that there are so many well-known stars in the Seniors. It's a built-in advantage. And to stay in the Seniors you have to win a certain amount of money each year so you know you've got big winners playing against big winners, which almost always guarantees a good show.

I think that another big part of the appeal of those Legends of Golf TV shows is that they show so much more *golf*. Not all that boring junk you're usually forced to watch on a televised golf program. You know . . . the blimp flying over, the pretty scenery, somebody hitching his pants up or walking down the fairway. In The Legends they show *golf shots*. Isn't that what people want to see?

Maybe because we've all been playing so long (this is my fifty-second year as a pro), we make sure that we put on golf shows for golf nuts. You know, the people who can watch it from dawn to dusk and who appreciate the artistry of it. Knowing you've got people like that watching, you've got a responsibility to show the whole field. In a big tournament with a lot of players, each part of your audience is rooting for its own man. A lot of people—when their man is in contention on most golf shows—rightfully complain, Where's *our* guy? They haven't shown him once. And look, now they're showing the leader just walking up to the fairway, doing nothing. We'd like to see our guy hit a shot or two. . . .

These are true fans. But those television directors seem to keep the camera trained on somebody not be-

cause he's leading, or near to leading, or even not leading at all, but just because he's the most famous.

I know I like to watch a guy's performance no matter
when he is on or off the leader board. You can learn
from a player even when he's not winning.

Take Rod Monday. I call that man "the best player
who never won anything." He never even finished in the
money. He would work all summer saving up money so
he could go on the tour, and then he'd have one stroke
of rotten luck after another. It was like some old woods
witch laid a curse on him.

I remember one tournament where Rod was using a
caddy who was also a big fan of his. This kid knew
what a good player Rod was and wished more than
anything for him to win just one little trophy to prove
it. Nothing was going to convince this kid that any kind
of jinx was going to stop his hero.

Rod had just birdied 17 and actually had a chance.
This kid says, "Rod, you only have to have par on the
last hole to win this tournament!"

Rod doesn't bat an eye. "Something will happen," he
says. "Always has."

The kid says, "No, Rod, boy, you're playing super.
Even if you make a bogey, you'll still come in second."

Rod says, "Something'll happen."

Kid says, "No, you'll hit a beauty."

So Rod hit a big drive out there, and the kid said
"attaboy."

Then Rod threw up some grass on a four-iron shot
and hooked it, and the wind carried it over into the
bunker.

"That's all right," says the kid. "You're the best

bunker player I ever saw, you can just zip it up there."

So Rod sends the kid up to hold the flag. Under the then rules, when your ball landed within sixty feet of the hole you had to have the flag held, or take it out. Rod must have decided to let the kid be up there when the ball rolled in. So that kid just scampered up there and held that flag so proudly, you'd think it was the trophy already won.

Rod walked into that trap, worked his feet down into the sand and made a beautiful swing. The ball arced out, took one bounce and was all set to stop right at the hole.

Except meanwhile this kid was having a problem getting the flag out of the hole. It was stuck; anyway, it wouldn't come out. The kid saw the ball coming and must have gotten desperate, because he reached down and gave that flag a jerk with all his might.

Well sir, the flagpole pops out just as Rod's winning ball is coming and smacks that ball up into the air, sending it flying back onto the fairway about 50 yards.

You couldn't see any expression on Rod's face as he stood there in the sand bunker. He just looked down and then smoothed his footprints out in the sand.

The caddy's got the palsy now because he knows he's cost Rod two shots.

Rod says, "C'mon, caddy, give me a club." He went back down and played it back up to the green and took three putts.

As he walked off the green this kid has got tears in his eyes. "Gosh, Rod, that's about the worst break I ever saw anybody get in their entire life."

Rod said, "That's okay, I knew it was going to happen all the time."

That Rod is the dadgonedest guy I ever saw in my life. He must've had some kind of black cloud hanging over his head. It was his defeatist attitude. I've always tried to keep the opposite attitude and I've been lucky. My luck is coming on when I feel an elation coming over me, a special feeling. It comes with a feeling of lightness in my fingers. I can feel a hair if it drops on my finger. My senses sharpen up, concentration sharpens up. As I play I can feel myself getting pumped up until I feel like I'm going to explode—or like I'm walking on air.

Once the opposite happened, and I didn't know what to do about it. I was playing with Ben Hogan at Pinehurst for the North and South, and out of the blue I felt myself letting down. I wasn't tired at the time, I can't tell you what the problem was. The air was just coming right out of my balloon. I thought to myself, Hey, I've got to get pumped up here. I've noticed the same thing in other players. My nephew, J. C., had it. At the Doral he was coming into the 18th hole and I could tell that all the air had come out of him and he just wanted to run. If a rabbit had come through at that moment, he'd have run off with it. He really wanted to go. But then he just forced himself to get pumped up again, and he clinched it. When you get pumped up like that, you can hit the ball farther than you normally do. When you can feel that it's going to zip like that, you have to allow for it and usually slide back a club.

When I shot 61 in 1936 at Greenbrier, I was coming into the 18th and I was real pumped up. Sense told me to take the shot nice and easy, but when I got to the tee it just seemed like I exploded. God, I hit that thing. In all the years afterward I never got pumped that high on that hole again, and as a result I never was able to hit a ball that far there ever again, although I played the course many times.

My body had taken over on that shot, a phenomenon that happens to many golfers—pro and amateur. Sense dictates you hit the ball one way, but instinct, like a little angel sitting on your shoulder, whispers to you at the last possible second. I remember one time I had just missed a six-footer on the 17th hole. It popped into the hole, right center, then just curled right out again. Oh, man!

Coming onto the 18th at Greenbrier I was trying to reason with myself. Don't be too mad. All you've got to do is make par for a 61. I hit a good drive out to the fairway, then used my five-iron to put it onto the green. I was dying to make my putt, but my amateur partners were arguing about who was going to shoot first.

Meanwhile I'm looking at the lay of my ball and I'm making myself crazy trying to decide whether it looks like it has more break or less break, whether I'd need to tap it or spank it. On and on these guys argued until finally I said, "Hey fellas, let me get at this thing, okay?"

At the moment I finally hit the ball, that little angel on my shoulder whispered to me that I was going to leave the ball below the hole. So *as I'm putting,* my arms adjust, and I hit it just that itty bit harder. It went through just like that and caught left center of the hole and dropped in. If I had hit the ball the way I was going to, it would have leaked right out. That's the kind of situation where a really fine touch is everything.

That's the biggest problem of the older player, keeping a fine touch. The first thing that starts to go is your short game, and that's the last thing you learn. Some people never become good putters. Look at Dick Metz. That man had a beautiful golf game, played like hell from tee to green, but then . . . forget it.

Golf is two games, played in two ways and in two places. The first game is played by hitting your ball through the air. The second is played by rolling your ball on the ground. Some people have the nerve and the ability to roll it on the ground. It doesn't take any strength to speak of, but it takes mind, concentration, and muscle control.

It must be some kind of divine joke, but a golfer's hands are the first things that start to tremor and shake. Golfers are always straining their backs, and it's in the back where the hand nerves start. From there they run to your arms and out to your fingertips. A doc told me, "You guys injure those nerves from all those years of twisting."

What he didn't say is that it starts to get to you mentally, too. Even if you're playing a green that's absolutely dead flat, no breaks or changes in the grass and no slopes to make the ball run off to the right or to the left . . . even then it starts to get to you. First you find yourself sweating it and saying, I don't know whether I can make this or not—this is really getting tough. And then all of a sudden you find yourself saying, No way is this ball going in there. Your mind plays tricks on you; you find yourself saying, It looks like there's a ridge going down to that hole and it looks like the ball is going on one side of that ridge . . . or the other.

And you do it to yourself. I've seen guys in the Seniors shiver and shake on the green, facing a ball that's resting there pretty as you please on a perfectly flat surface.

Partly it's nerve control, partly it's in the head. I can't begin to tell you how many people putt "sidesaddle" now. When you get to the point that your nerves go, if you still play fairly well and like to play, you've got to swallow a little of your pride. Sidesaddle looks awful, but not as awful as watching somebody try to putt when they've got an acute case of the yips. When some of these players putt, the club actually trembles against the ball. It happened when I was playing with President Gerald Ford. He had a one-foot putt that . . . I don't know how many times he hit it on the way to the hole.

I double-hit them myself something horrible. My moment of truth came in the early 1960s when I was playing in the PGA. I double-hit one on the 10th hole in front of all those people. I couldn't keep my fingers from shaking. Well, that was it. I took a great big swallow and down went my pride. On the next hole I turned around and putted between my legs, and I stayed that way . . . until they changed the rules and you couldn't putt like that. That's when I developed my sidesaddle putt.

Because of the yips, which come partly from nerve damage and partly from the natural aging process, putting is the part of the game where you can really see a player's age. Cary Middlecoff said that's why he quit. When he was playing out there in The Legends, he said, "I was giving my man about one and a half putts a round, and that's not the way the game is supposed to be played."

Yds.	Par	Hcp.	Hole	Sam Snead				W. Par
389	4	7	1	3				4
120	3	17	2	3				3
412	4	3	3	3				5
372	4	9	4	3				4
367	4	11	5	4				4
293	4	15	6	3				4
409	4	1	7	4				5
391	4	5	8	4				4
286	4	13	9	4				4
3039	35		OUT	31				37
The "GREENBRIER" Course								
236	3	14	10	3				3
435	4	4	11	4				5
400	4	10	12	3				5
395	4	12	13	3				4
174	3	18	14	2				3
483	5	6	15	3				5
526	5	2	16	4				5
200	3	16	17	3				3
439	4	8	18	3				5
3288	35		IN	28				38
6327	70		TOT.	59				75
HANDICAP						DATE		
NET SCORE								

THE GOLF AND TENNIS CLUB
Focal point of The Greenbrier's three golf courses

The "GREENBRIER" Course

Ditches on 2, 3, 10, 12, 14 and 16 fairways are water hazards.
Ball driven from the 15th tee landing in the road may be dropped back without penalty. Ditch left of 5th and 6th fairways is a parallel hazard.

To expedite course play, please give way to faster matches.

Unless otherwise specified, U.S.G.A. rules apply.

MATCH PLAY (Three-fourths of Medal Play)

WHITE SULPHUR SPRINGS, WEST VIRGINIA

SAM SNEAD, GOLF PROFESSIONAL

The scorecard for my 59 game, May 16, 1959. Credit: The Greenbrier

I'm admiring my Izett driver that Henry Picard (center) sold me for $5.50. I used it for 30 years—through most of my national tournament wins. Greenbrier Manager Fred Martin is on the right.

Me with my dog Bucky at my home in Highland Beach, Florida.

Gene Sarazen, me and Jimmy Demaret in Colorado. Credit: Shell's Wonderful World of Golf.

Byron Nelson and I were born just a few months apart in 1912, but we were both still in contention in 1976 at the Riviera. Credit: Lester C. Nehamkin.

Demonstrating my controversial "sidesaddle" putt. Credit: Time Inc.

Somehow they caught me without my hat, with Billy Casper (left) and Lee Trevino. Credit: Lester C. Nehamkin.

Still competing in 1986 with some of the best guys in golf: (front, left to right) Doug Sanders, Bob Goalby and Gay Brewer. (Back, left to right) Billy Casper, me and Doug Ford.

My own short game has changed a lot, even since I went onto the Senior Tour. Over the last four years, since my eyes went, my chipping has been just awful. I have no depth perception now. But if I know how far I have to pitch it, to carry it through the air, I can hit it from memory. It's like an airplane pilot making an instrument landing. Instead of relying on gauges and the air traffic controller, a golfer has to depend on a caddy. If the caddy tells me it's 90 yards or 100 yards, I can ping it there pretty close. I just look and say, I've got to hit this thing 100 yards. Then it's just a matter of muscle memory.

Craig Wood had the ability to hit the ball and make it go straight from the club; no hook, no fade. I think he hit the ball straightest of anybody. I wish I knew where he got his control. His putting especially made me green with envy.

Some people say putting is ninety percent confidence, or ninety percent mental. I don't know what percent it is. I do believe, however, that a putter must start with the ability to make some kind of controlled stroke. The next thing in putting is speed. You can mishit a putt, but if you have the right speed it can go in anyway. Yips or not, if you don't have a controlled stroke, if you find yourself hitting one to the right, one to the left, one too hard, one too soft, if your speed fluctuates . . . then you're not likely to hole many putts.

The Seniors is full of guys who have long games that are a work of art; but where their short games are concerned, to quote Rod Monday, "all the wheels fall off, even the spare."

*   *   *

THE ISSUE OF age is causing a row in the Seniors, and it's just going to get worse. For one thing there's a big controversy over who is getting the money. That's infuriating, especially for those of us who got the thing off the ground. I guess I was born a little too soon: Too old when the good money came in on the regular tour *and* too old now that the Senior tour's starting to come on strong.

The problem is simple: All the big stars of the sixties and seventies are coming in, and they're winning the pots and pushing us older players out. The way things are going, it's not going to be the Seniors anymore. They'll keep calling it the Seniors, but actually it's going to wind up being a club for golfers age 50 to about 57. There won't be any over-60-year-olds. They'll just root us all out.

There's very little difference in a golfer's game between age 40 and 45. There's a little more difference between 45 and 50. Between 50 and 55 there's a good bit of difference, and between 55 and 60 there's a helluva lot of difference. After that . . .

Well, I'm 74 and still competing, but it takes every minute of work I can give it. I've done all right. I won The Legends again in 1980, paired with Don January, and the Newport Commemorative the same year, but it's getting harder to compete against the younger guys. They know it, too, and they're not out to make it any easier.

For example, who would have thought that a fuss

over a side issue like golf carts would tear up the Seniors? We've been using carts to get around the course because, hell, we're the Seniors and it makes life a little easier.

But now we've got these 50-year-olds coming off the regular PGA tour, and they're used to walking around the course. They say we shouldn't allow carts. To me, it looks like maybe they're trying to shove us older guys overboard and take the big purses for themselves. Sooner or later I suppose the other younger guys will have their way and there will be no more carts in the Seniors, which will discourage a lot of the over-60s even more. But they should keep in mind that it won't be so long before those carts are going to look pretty good to them, too. Time marches on. . . .

When Chick Harbert became fifty, somebody said, "Hey Chick, oh boy, now that you're fifty you're going to tear up that Seniors." Chick said, "Hell, I couldn't beat Snead when I was twenty-one, I don't know if I got any better chance now." That was nice of him, but mother nature is Mother Nature. I know I'm getting older but I also know that I'll be damned if I'll give up playing, even if I get to be a hundred. We were sitting around talking about it, kind of half-joking that we should start a new tournament and keep out anybody under seventy. But that gave me an idea.

In July 1986 I incorporated something I call "The Major Champions of Golf." It's only for players sixty and older. The idea is simple: we're making ourselves available as a group for the first time in our careers to be guest pros at corporate outings—I mentioned those earlier—to raise money for charity. We went public in August with one ad in the *Wall Street Journal* with my name in it, and the response was pretty fantastic. We've gotten requests for dates from businesses and charities, large and small, all over the country.

I hope to be available for as many events as I can get to. It turns out that there are a lot of people out there who say they would just love to have fifteen or twenty older name pros come and play with a group of them. Usually those conventions don't run more than a hundred people, so we figure we're able to parcel out one pro to every four or so of the participants. We've got an impressive lineup of talent. The Major Champions of Golf is just that: a very enthusiastic group of people who have won the major championships—the British Open, the U.S. Open, the Masters and the PGA. I'm president, Julius Boros is vice president, Jack Fleck is secretary and Doug Ford is treasurer.

Not only does it please a lot of the old-time fans, it will help us older pros stay in the Seniors a little longer. For some it will be the only way they can stay on the tour at an advanced age. You take Ford, Jerry Barber, Fleck, Freddy Haas, guys like that—they can't make much more than expenses on the tours. They come out every week and support the Senior tour, but they're getting down into that lower income bracket. I've slipped a bit in winnings myself since beginning the tour in 1980, but the competitive fire is still there.

It makes no sense to discourage older pros. Look what the Seniors has done to encourage older players all over the country to keep on playing. Look what it did for Miller Barber, Gay Brewer, and such players. Among the general public I think it's created a new interest in the sport. With all the new medical techniques, people are living longer and that's good. To keep healthy, older people have got to exercise. Golf is the best damn exercise I know, no matter *what* your age. And unlike football or baseball or even tennis, you can keep at it most of your life. I'd like to think that seeing me and the others golfing will inspire older people all over the country to get out and get around doing *something,* even if it's not golf. And maybe it will encourage some of the older golfers, the ones who have put away their clubs, to come out of retirement. Ben Hogan and Byron Nelson and I were all born in 1912, but both of them have stopped playing competitively. As things are now, Hogan and Nelson couldn't play the Senior tour today; they wouldn't qualify. They couldn't play because they haven't won enough money to qualify. It's crazy.

Speaking of Ben Hogan, I haven't seen him in four or five years. The last time was at Augusta at the Masters. With all the stories of the great rivalry, we were actually pretty friendly. But really, *nobody* knew Ben Hogan. When people say they're close to Hogan or they know this or that about him—I say that's just not true. Demaret was as close to him, I suppose, as any of us. I asked him about Hogan once, and even he said, "I can't really say I know the man."

The only one who knows the real Hogan is his wife, Valerie, but she and Ben are by themselves in their house in Fort Worth, Texas. Oh, it's a huge place, and beautiful, but I understand they have no guests. Who knows why? Anyway—it's kind of sad, because Ben Hogan is a great man.

He never talked on the golf course and didn't have much to say off it either. He's been consistent there.

Here's typical Hogan: Claude Harmon was playing with Hogan at the Masters in Augusta. On the 12th hole Harmon makes a hole-in-one. A hole-in-one at the Masters! A big cheer went up and everybody applauded. Then the two of them walk up to the green together but Hogan doesn't say anything. Hogan putts, makes a birdy 2, doesn't say a thing. They walk to the 13th, tee off, and finally Hogan says, "What'd you have back there, Claude?" Harmon says, "I had a one, Ben," and he waits to see Hogan's reaction. But Hogan goes right on like nothing happened.

It's not that he begrudged Harmon the shot, he was just already involved in concentrating on his own next shot. To him, Claude's one was just one stroke less than his two.

Oh, there are stories about how Ben wouldn't recognize his own wife on the golf course, how he'd be almost in a trance. The point is that he concentrated so hard that he just didn't see anybody or anything and didn't want anybody to talk to him or break his concentration.

Hogan's career ended at the 16th hole of the Masters. His putting seemed to leave him right then and there, and that was the end of one of the most glorious careers in the game. Left it flat. Now he won't even play in public. In private he plays a game we call "greenies": knock it on the green, take a putter, and knock it off.

Outside of the great cart controversy and the way some of the older players are being treated, I've got no serious complaint with the Seniors committee. They're just trying to do their job, although sometimes the players think they haven't placed the pros right or given somebody the right pairing.

Pairing is important. No question, there are some guys I'd rather play with than others, and I'm sure some guys would just as soon skip a pairing with me. You like a man's game to be like yours. Some have a nice easy tempo, some are erratic and don't get the job done. I'd rather play with a man who shoots low rounds—though not as low as mine, of course. In general I prefer somebody who has a nice rhythm to his swing, someone whose timing is good, not jerky. Some guys get real nervous, yips or no, and their actions are quick and annoying. Some guys talk so much you want to pop a few balls in their mouth to cork up the noise. When you get paired with somebody who distracts you like that, you just have to try to keep away from him.

EXCEPT FOR MY work in Major Champions, I don't plan to give lessons anymore. People call, asking for them, but I'm not a teaching pro at any club now. I was a pro at The Greenbrier for thirty years. Now, as you know, I represent Gleneagles and The Homestead. At The Homestead, in Hot Springs, they don't have driving ranges so you have to shag your own balls. At its number one course, The Cascades, you don't have a place to practice, so sometimes I go down and warm up on the

16th fairway. It's a fine course, though, one of the best in the South.

I signed on at Gleneagles in 1984 and they opened the course in 1985, but I'm not the club pro. That's Lew Hersey—a fun guy to be around and a great pro for the members. As for me, I'm just one of the six touring pros who represent Gleneagles as we travel around. The others are Billy Casper, Bob Goalby, Doug Ford, Doug Sanders and Gay Brewer. We six pros made a number of recommendations to the club's architect, most of which were carried out. That's one of the advantages of having six experienced touring pros on the staff.

Gleneagles keeps the course nicely and they've promised to have it in tiptop condition for the November 1986 Seniors tournament. . . . Speaking of well-conditioned courses, I think that Pine Tree in Boynton Beach, Florida is as fine a golf course as I ever played, and I bet most golfers would say the same.

I'VE SOMETIMES MADE an exception and tried to help some of the pros. Take Ralph Guldahl, for example. Ralph always was a strong player and he beat me more than once, but I think I was able to give him some useful advice.

I played a lot of exhibitions with Ralph during my first years on the tour so I knew his swing. He didn't go into the service during World War II, but staying a civilian didn't help his hitting much. When I came back after the war I heard talk that he couldn't hit his hat.

We were playing together in Portland, Oregon, where I had a chance to see his problem first hand. I went up to him and called him by his nickname. "Goldie," I said, "I'll bet you've played more golf with me than anybody you ever played with. I know your swing pretty well. Now, if you want me to help you sometime . . ."

He waved me away. "Aw, I'll get it," he said.

He tried studying photos and movies of his swing and did a lot of practicing, but nothing much helped. Finally his wife told him, "Give Sam a try."

So I took him and fixed his hands around the club. Goldie tried my new grip a few times and said, "It doesn't feel right."

I said, "Well, I wouldn't think it would. That grip is the one you used when you were winning everything in sight. Now you've gotten away from it and you're doing something new—and that something new is *wrong.*"

That sort of thing happens a lot with older players. You start playing with your feet turned in a certain direction, and over the years you slip into something that may be more comfortable but isn't giving you the bracing you need at a crucial moment. If you try turning it back the way it used to be, it won't feel as comfortable. But it may help your game. As far as old Ralph Guldahl was concerned, his grip was the bugaboo that was wrecking his whole game.

I'm proud to say that I also was able to help Joanne Carner, who at one time was the top money winner on the LPGA tour. She had been taking lessons from another pro, and one day her husband, Don, came to me and said he didn't think the other pro could do her any more good, and would I look at Joanne.

After one session working with me, she won four tournaments in a row. She was so pleased that as soon as she got a moment off the tour she drove all the way back to Hot Springs for lesson number two. She's one of the most natural athletes I've ever seen. After that she won two more, bam bam.

More recently Tom Watson came to me at the Masters and told me Curtis Strange wasn't hitting the way he used to. I was tempted, because a request like that is an honor. But my philosophy is changing. Now I tell people, "Everybody has his own way of doing it." The most I say is, "Well, your timing is off a little bit." Or, "You used to do it this way and now you're doing it the other way."

I'm not trying to be smart. It's my firm belief that there is such a thing as getting too much pro'd. I mean, you can get so overloaded with professional advice and theories and rules that you don't know *what* to do next.

My nephew J. C. is an offender in that department. I think in a few minutes I could have him hitting the ball like you shoot a gun, but I can't get him to sit still and listen to one line of advice. He'd rather listen to every other Tom, Dick and Harry who hangs up his shingle and says, "I'm a pro."

J. C. and I have a funny relationship. He has to walk around with my name hanging on him, which can't be too comfortable. He and I are always trying to tell each other what to do, and trying to see who's the better golfer. We were paired together at one of my favorite places—the PGA championship at Oakland Hills. I only came in third, but I was in my sixties and there aren't too many players that age who can land in the money on the regular tour—and in one of the majors. It was my last real chance for a national title, but I consoled myself with the thought that this old man had just beat his own nephew!

When we started out, J. C. was ribbing me. "You're not going to hit that low shitty fade of yours, are you?" And I said, "Well, I do plan to be on the fairway."

But before we played nine holes I was doing so well that he seemed to forget about his own game and started coaching me! Coming in, he was telling me, "Now watch where you're aiming, now look out for that bunker, now don't get that thing past that hole . . ." J. C. became a cheerleader and a regular backseat golfer.

At the 10th, my ball stopped one inch from the center of the hole. At the 11th, it did the same thing. Then I 3-putted 13, and said, "Man, if I'd saved those three shots, I'd have tied!" But it wasn't so, because I bogeyed the next couple of holes.

Even though I was in my sixties, it's no surprise that I scored that well in the PGA tournament. I was playing well enough from tee to green. I think I can beat most of these guys in the Seniors from tee to green right now. But you've got to get it in the hole. You put it in there five feet from the hole, praying for a birdie—your opponent drives it into the trash, knocks it into the bunker, knocks it fifteen feet out on the green, and *finally* knocks it into the hole for a par four. You start with a five foot putt for a birdie, three-putt, make a bogey, and lose a stroke to a guy who hits three bad shots! You gotta know how that feels. You go like that for a few holes, you just want to pack it in. You start to think, "If only I had a good deep hole where I could throw everything, nobody would ever find it."

EVERY GOLFER WILL tell you that the short game is the killer, but there have been times when my long game was all I needed.

I've hit twenty-nine holes-in-one in my career. I had two of them in 1984, when I was 72. I made one in a friendly game in Philadelphia, and one in tournament play in Lexington, Kentucky. That Kentucky hole-in-one was one of those instrument landings. It was on an elevated green that I couldn't even see. I just aimed for the flag, smacked that ball, and all of a sudden a big squall goes up in the crowd behind the green.

Before that, I hit them in Sacramento, Cincinnati, Austin, Texas—all over the map. In The Legends of Golf I made one at Onion Creek and they sent me a *chair* as a trophy. Was that a hint?

I once hit a ball so hard that when we came up to the green all we could see was a big dent about six feet in front of the cup. That little ball was hiding right down inside the hole like it was trying to avoid getting blamed for the damage. I also hit one at Cherry Hill in Denver, playing with a fellow named Fred Manning, and after I hit the ball I saw the flag give a little jerk.

"That's a hole-in-one," I said, as we went over to the green.

Manning said, "It can't be."

So we walked down the fairway. There was only one ball on the green, and Manning said, "Sam, that's my ball there. You didn't get any hole-in-one. You're down behind the green somewhere."

I said, "No, it's in there. Caddy, would you get my ball out of the hole?"

Manning said, "Don't bother, son, he's off in a bunker somewhere."

I said, "Would you just look to make sure."

So he walked up to the cup, bent over, and all I heard was Manning . . . "Well, I'll be damned."

I'D LOVE TO make one more try at the U.S. Open, but I'd have to qualify, and I don't think I can do that now. I content myself with slugging it out in the Seniors. I think my best game on the Senior tour was when I beat Julius Boros for the PGA Seniors by fifteen shots down in Florida. His wife followed him around and she couldn't believe what she saw. Afterwards she told me, "I thought we were playing a different course."

I have a lot of good memories like that. And my memory, luckily, is pretty good. A guy said to me once, "Mr. Snead, my hat is off to you. You hit the greatest shot that I ever saw. It was down in New Orleans, though I couldn't tell you the year."

"On the eighteenth hole?" I asked.

"Yeah!"

"The one that banks to the right?"

"Yeah!"

"A par five? I cut a three-wood about six feet?"

"That's right."

"Yeah, and then I missed the putt."

"That's right!"

He remembered the shot, but I remembered how I shot it. Certain shots, you remember. A lot of them you want to forget . . . and can't.

Aside from times I get the yips, I think my saddest moment came in the Jacksonville Open—the time Doug Ford and I were tied, and I thought I needed to birdie the last two holes to win. On the 17th, my putt rolled by the cup by about three and a half feet. By the time I came to the last hole, I thought I'd lost, but instead I found that I'd tied Ford and was facing a sudden death playoff.

On the first hole he put it in a fairway bunker. On the second he put it in the lake. Things were looking hopeful, but then when I was on the green counting the winnings in my head, he proceeded to chip right into the hole. I missed my putt and he won the tournament.

I've lost more than one tournament by not knowing the right score. Plenty of times I've been told that my opponent was in front of me with such-and-such a number, and it turned out to be false. When you think you're behind, you play one way. When you think you're ahead, you play another. Getting the wrong advice makes you play the wrong shots. And that, all too often, is disaster.

I had a caddy once who told me all I had to do was

2-putt the green. My shot hung on the lip. I heard people roar up ahead while I was trying to make the four, and learned my opponent and I were really tied. He beat me on the first extra hole.

One big improvement in tournament play today is that you can always see a leader board. That's useful for lots of reasons, including knowing what's going on behind you as well as ahead.

SO FAR I'VE had a lot of fun in the Seniors PGA. I had my lowest score when I was playing Skip Alexander. He's got a white beard and white hair and he used to make fun of my bald scalp. The first round I shot 66, he shot 80. Even though he was virtually eliminated, he stuck around to watch me. "Nudie," he said, "I just thought I'd stay over and see if you could do that again."

So, I shot 66 again.

On the next round I had two pars left for what looked like another 66, but then I 3-putted the 17th and ended with a 67.

That Saturday night I dreamed that I was going to par the first ten holes the next day, and then birdie four in a row. The dream was so vivid that I could smell the grass and see the break in the greens. I think my spirit went wandering out on that course that night and played the game while all of us were asleep.

Well, don't get the creeps, but do you know that the next morning I shot par on the first ten holes, and then I punched one after another—birdie, birdie, birdie— three in a row.

But when I came to the easiest hole, the par-four 14th —damn, but I couldn't make that other birdie. I had makeable birdie putts from there on in, but I just couldn't seem to get them down. I finally shot 66-66-67-69—what you almost might call my "dream" game.

I wish I was shooting like that today. I try to hit my age, and even though I'm seventy-four, I'm far from the worst player in the Seniors. Right now I'd say the *best* player in the Seniors is Gary Player. He's top of the board. Dale Douglas is good, too, and Bruce Crampton's playing well. Chi-Chi Rodriguez is the top money winner in the Seniors. Watching Chi-Chi play today, you shake your head. He's really managed to hold his game together—a great guy.

The guy I'm waiting to see in the Seniors is Jack Nicklaus. Jack's a friendly guy, and a great player. I've beaten him, though not in tournament play. Our ages don't exactly coincide. I played him at Loxahatchie in Florida in early 1986, a few months before his big Masters win. Ed Tutweiler and I played him and his son, and I'm proud to say we won, 4 up and 3 to play.

Like I said, Nicklaus gave all us older guys a charge when he won the Masters in April 1986. I saw his win on television. I was at the tournament in person on Thursday and played nine holes with Sarazen, but then decided to watch the last round on TV.

TV is, of course, important to golf today—it helps keep your profile high, keep your face in front of the public, which can have a short memory, especially for golfers.

But nothing helps like winning a big tournament. My

age be hanged, I plan to return to more tournament playing if my right eye improves. And of course there's my new Major Champions of Golf. I like spending time with all those guys I started out with. I think we had more fun then than they have now on the regular tour. We didn't do anything strange after a round, but we had fun.

NOW THAT I'M getting older, you'd think Mrs. Snead would ask me to stay home more, put my feet up. And you'd be right.

"What are you doing out there?" she says. "You're not beating anybody. Why don't you stay home and save your money?"

Well, it's like anything else, it pays to advertise. At least as long as I keep my name in front of the public, we'll sell some more Wilson golf clubs—but of course that's not the only reason.

Audrey says to me, "Haven't you made enough money?"

I say, "How much is enough?" And I say it with a straight face.

Not many people know this, but Mrs. Snead is a golfer too. Audrey doesn't come from a golf family . . . her people didn't know one club from another. But for that matter, neither did my dad at first. Audrey won the Boca Raton Club Women's Championship twice. She was an eight handicap. We've played together, and I'm not ashamed to say that Mrs. Snead is a very good competitor. We fish together sometimes too.

At one point my wife wasn't playing too well, and she asked me to give her a lesson. Her left arm was coming away from her body at the top of her swing, and I said, "What the hell are you doing?" She was almost looking under her arm at the ball.

I said, "You've got to keep your left arm right up against your left titty, all the way back up there."

She tried that, and she started hitting the ball just like old times. Even with her eight handicap Audrey would beat those gals down there that were a two. There's no question that she was the better player. When we were in high school together, she was a guard on the basketball team. I refereed a game or two, and I'll tell you she stuck right to her man like a leech. Those gals didn't get near that ball.

I had gone out with her in high school but I wouldn't say she was my steady girlfriend. After high school I went out on the tour, and she and I kind of broke up for a while.

When I turned pro, I never will forget, I was eating in a restaurant and somebody came up to me and said, "Somebody wants to see you." I went outside and there was Audrey, sitting in a car with one of her girl friends. I got in and talked to her, and pretty soon we were starting our romance all over again. We got married in 1940, in August. There were only two other people at the ceremony, Nelson Long—he was the best man—and his wife. We left the church and drove to Cumberland, Maryland, and spent the night there. The next day we set out for Niagara Falls for a combination honeymoon/golfing trip. I had my eye on the Canadian Open and figured, Well, as long as we're in the neighbor-hood . . .

Needless to say, Audrey got used to the idea of me golfing PDQ. She followed me on the tour some until 1944, then we had the first child and she'd come along for a week or two at a time, but that's tough when you've got a babe in arms.

Audrey's a leader, and she's strong-minded. She doesn't take a back seat to anybody. We've never dis-cussed Women's Liberation and such, but take it from me that she could give me a hard time when she wanted to.

One night we're watching TV and an announcer came on, talking about President Kennedy. Someone had done a story, claimed that Kennedy had a thousand women.

I said to Audrey, "Isn't that the worst trash you ever heard? Here's the poor man dead and in his grave, and these people are going around saying he's had a thou-sand women."

So Audrey turned to me. "Oh yeah? You had *two* thousand before you met me!"

That's not true, of course, but I said, "Thank you very much. Guy sure did miss a lot, didn't he?"

Women? —There have always been a lot of women around the golf tour; it's just a matter of how you act toward them. We used to play up in St. Paul every year, one of the few tournaments that had women keeping score. They tried to get a lot of attractive gals, and some of the guys wound up marrying those pretty scorekeep-ing gals up there in St. Paul. As a result, a lot of the married guys' wives wouldn't let them go play in St. Paul if they couldn't go along with them.

That was a nice little town, St. Paul. It wasn't very cold when we'd go up there, but it was mighty lonely for a single man on the road. Those gals were temptations, that's for sure, but the reaction would depend on the individual golfer. If a man was looking for something, well, it wasn't very hard to find. But a lot of us weren't looking for anything. A gal could say, "Come on," and the best way to handle it would be to say, all innocent, "Who are you?"

We had some Puritans up there, and we had some . . . well, the reverse. Some of them wouldn't even make their tee-off times.

Another part of the situation with women was that we were a lot closer to the crowd in the old days. Things were a lot more intimate. They didn't have the courses roped off, so people could get right up next to you all the time. They could reach right out and touch you, and believe me, they did.

It wasn't as pleasant as it might sound. People'd surround you and horseshoe you in. A lot of times I'd hit the shot, and they'd take off in such a stampede that they'd knock the club right out of my hand. I never got to see the ball; I never knew whether it got on the green or where it went.

IN THOSE DAYS we used plain balls and wooden clubs. When I started they were just beginning to introduce steel shafts. The first steel shaft was perforated, to make it light enough to swing. The only problem is that when you'd swing one, it'd go *whhhsh*. A hell of a sound. Then they came out with a candied shaft with a yellow plastic sheath. The equipment has changed a lot since I started in 1934. There's no question the clubs are better now. The ball has improved tremendously—we played with the small ball before they went up to the larger regulation ball.

I played with every kind of ball back then . . . with the feather, the Haskell, the gutta-percha. The gutta-perchas started out smooth as could be, and every time you'd whop it, it'd get a dent. But we soon discovered that the more dents, the better it flew. So you'd see golfers punching holes in the balls, cutting them, even pounding them with hammers.

The only problem was, they weren't very durable. If your gutta-percha ball broke, regulations said you had to play the biggest piece. Putting one of those chunks could get right rough.

To get those balls ready to tee up, you had a little box of sand and a bucket of water at each tee. You'd wet the ball to clean it off, then roll it in the sand to dry it out before putting it on the tee. If you addressed that ball and it fell off the tee, you had to play it, and that counted as a stroke. They've changed the rules, of course, and now if it falls off the tee, you just tee it up again.

GOLF IS IN my blood and I'll never shake it. But also in my blood, as you must gather by now, is the desire to hunt and fish. I try to find time to do both.

I've been living in Florida for about a thousand years now, but they've built a new house for me at Gleneagles, which I moved into last spring. I plan to do some fishing in the backyard pond . . . it looks like I've got thousands of little bitty ones in there now. That's one of the things I love about Florida. No matter what pond it is in Florida, it'll eventually have fish in it. They don't have to stock it. Birds eat the fertilized eggs or carry them in there on their legs or feet. They'll be maybe trash fish, but you'll have them. And if you put three or four thousand bass in there, boy, they'd grow like nobody's business with all that fry in there.

I've gotten to the point where I don't like to kill stuff anymore. I've had deer come within a foot of me, but my wife won't cook it, so there's doubly no sense in my killing it.

I do hunt turkey, though. Those turkeys can be smart. I heard that eighty percent of them die of old age. Deer are much smarter, though. If you put a deer and a turkey in a wooded area, you'd get the turkey nine out of ten times.

I TRY TO spend time with my thirteen-year-old grandson, Samuel Jackson Snead III. His only problem is, he's got no one to play golf with. Boys have got to have someone to compete with. They've got to have someone they can beat or can't beat or are trying to beat.

BATH IS NEXT to the smallest county in Virginia. We're the only one that doesn't have a stop light. I'm one local boy who left town and came back, if I may say so, a winner. And if I had it all to do over again, I'd do it the same way.

Well, there are some shots I'd do over. And I sure wouldn't mind winning the U.S. Open, just once. But that's something you can never get back.

I'm not complaining. I'm tied with lowest round ever shot in the PGA—a 59. I hold the record for the last thirty-six holes—122. And I still hold the lowest stroke average for a year—69.2 for ninety-six straight rounds in 1950.

I've won more tournaments than anybody.

Some people say, "Well, Snead didn't win the U.S. Open."

True. But you can't let that beat the whole idea of a man's record. Nicklaus never won the L.A. Open or the Canadian Open. I won them both. Palmer never won the PGA. One's as hard to win as the other.

I try never to get discouraged, and I'd say the same to any 74-year-old golfer, even one who was just starting out.

I'd tell that man to get the fundamentals first, then *try*. If he gets the right fundamentals, it will make it a lot easier and he'll enjoy it more. And *enjoying*—that's what golf, and life, is all about.

Appendix

SAM SNEAD

Personal Data

Full Name: Samuel Jackson Snead

Height: 5'11"   **Weight:** 190

Birth Date: May 27, 1912

Birthplace: Hot Springs, VA

Residence: Hot Springs, VA

Family: Wife Audrey; children Sam Jr. (6-30-44), Terrance (5-27-52); two grandchildren.

Side Interests/Hobbies: Fishing, hunting.

Career Record

Turned Professional: 1934

Joined Tour: 1937   **Joined Senior Tour:** 1980

Career PGA Tour Earnings: $620,126

Playoffs: 8 (6 wins)

PGA Tour Victories:
1936—Virginia Closed Professional.

1937—St. Paul Open, Nassau Open, Miami Open, Oakland Open.

1938—Greensboro Open, Inverness Four-Ball, Goodall Round Robin, Chicago Open, Canadian Open, Westchester 108-Hole Open, White Sulphur Springs Open.

1939—Miami Open, St. Petersburg Open, Miami-Biltmore Four-Ball, Ontario Open.

1940—Inverness Four-Ball, Canadian Open, Anthracite Open.

1941—Canadian Open, St. Petersburg Open, North and South Open, Rochester *Times Union* Open, Henry Hurst Invitational.

1942—St. Petersburg Open, PGA, Cordoba Open.

1944—Richmond Open, Portland Open.

1945—Los Angeles Open, Gulfport Open, Pensacola Open, Jacksonville Open, Dallas Open, Tulsa Open.

1946—Miami Open, Greensboro Open, Jacksonville Open, Virginia Open, World Championship, British Open.

1948—Texas Open.

1949—Greensboro Open, PGA, Masters, Washington Star Open, Dapper Dan Open, Western Open.

1950—Texas Open, Miami Open, Greensboro Open, Inverness Four-Ball, North and South Open, Los Angeles Open, Colonial National Invitational, Reading Open.

1951—Miami Open, PGA.

1952—Inverness Four-Ball, Masters, Greenbrier Invitational, All-American, Eastern Open, Julius Boros Open.

1953—Texas Open, Greenbrier Invitational, Baton Rouge Open.

1954—Masters, PGA, Palm Beach Round Robin.

1955—Miami Open, Greensboro Open, Palm Beach
Round Robin, Insurance City Open.
1956—Greensboro Open.
1957—Dallas Open.
1958—Greenbrier Invitational.
1959—Sam Snead Festival.
1960—Greensboro Open, De Soto Open.
1961—Sam Snead Festival, Tournament of Champions.
1964—Haig and Haig Scotch Mixed Foursome Invitational.
1965—Greensboro Open.

Official Senior Career Earnings: $61,698

Outstanding Achievements of Senior Career:
1963, 1965, 1967, 1970, 1972, 1973—PGA Senior Champion.
1964, 1965, 1970, 1972, 1973—World Senior Champion.
1980—*Golf Digest* Pro-Am.
1978—Legends of Golf Winners (with Gardner Dickinson).
1980—Legends of Golf Winners (with Don January).

Other Achievements: Member of Ryder Cup team eight times, captain in 1951 and 1959, plus nonplaying captain in 1969. Chosen PGA Player of the Year in 1949. Won Vardon Trophy in 1938, 1949, 1950, 1955. Won World Cup individual title in 1961. Member of PGA and World Golf Halls of Fame. Tour's leading money winner in 1938, 1949 and 1950.
Credited with 135 victories by independent record-keepers and claims 165 himself, including regional events. Became oldest (52 years, 10

months) to win PGA tour event at 1965 Greensboro Open. Became first player in a PGA event to shoot his age—and better—when at age 67 he shot rounds of 67 and 66 in 1979 Quad Cities Open.

Club Affiliation: Represents The Cascades Golf and Tennis Club, Hot Springs, VA; Touring Professional, Gleneagles Country Club, Delray Beach, Florida.

Former Club Affiliation: Head Professional, The Greenbrier, White Sulphur Springs, WV, 1936–39 and 1947–74; Boca Raton Hotel and Beach Club, Boca Raton, FL.

Index

Abrams, Stan, 196
Alexander, Skip, 147, 221
Armour, Tommy, 99

Barber, Jerry, 171–72, 182, 210
Barber, Miller, 211
Bartlett, Charlie, 70
Berle, Milton, 130
Bernie, Ben, 152
Berry, Jim, 70
Bolger, Ray, 130, 131
Bolt, Tommy, 80, 93, 199
Boros, Julius, 182, 199, 210, 219
Bradley, Alva, 50–53, 56
Brewer, Gay, 196, 211
Brinkley, Horsehair, 120
Bulla, Johnny, 62–63, 67, 68–69, 102, 119
Burke, Billy, 48, 54, 55, 58
Burke, Jackie, 117
Burns, Fred, 57
Burns, Jimmy, 70

Carmichael, Hoagy, 135
Carner, Don, 215
Carner, Joanne, 215–16
Casper, Billy, 196
Cessna, Wally, 86

Como, Perry, 131
Cooper, Gary, 132
Cooper, Harry ("Lighthorse"), 70, 97, 99
Corcoran, Fred, 14, 65–66, 68–74, 77, 78, 79, 89, 91, 125, 126, 128, 129, 161–62
Crampton, Bruce, 182, 222
Crosby, Bing, 134–35
Cruickshank, Bobby, 59, 99

Demaret, Jimmy, 82, 97, 167, 198, 211
Dempsey, Jack, 136
DeVicenzo, Roberto, 199
Dickinson, Gardner, 199
Dietrich, Ken, 74–75
Douglas, Dale, 222
Dudley, Ed, 99, 103, 106, 108–9, 122

Eisenhower, President Dwight D. ("Ike"), 121–23, 124

Fazio, George, 60
Fisher, Johnny, 113
Fleck, Jack, 182, 210
Floyd, Raymond, 181

235

Flynn, Errol, 132
Ford, Doug, 148, 182, 196, 210, 220
Ford, President Gerald, 121, 206

Gagan, Steve, 50
Ghezzi, Vic, 97
Gleason, Jackie, 11, 133–34
Gleim, Freddy, 57–58
Goalby, Bob, 12, 159–60, 196
Goddard, Paulette, 132–33
Goodman, Johnny, 54, 55
Grainger, Ike, 164
Griffith, Andy, 132
Grisley, Doc, 44–45
Guldahl, Ralph ("Goldie"), 67, 83, 87, 97, 99, 100, 102, 106, 172, 214–15

Haas, Freddy, 210
Hagen, Walter, 59, 66, 82, 97, 160, 166–67, 183
Hammond, Speck, 66
Harbert, Chick, 209
Harmon, Claude, 212
Harney, Paul, 117
Harper, Chandler, 154
Heafner, Clayt, 155
Hemingway, Ernest, 135
Hersey, Lew, 214
Hill, Arthur, 124
Hines, Jimmy, 89
Hogan, Ben, 14, 15, 81, 91, 97, 99, 108, 135, 165–75, 180, 203, 211–12
Hogan, Valerie, 168, 170, 211

Holden, Bill, 130
Hope, Bob, 7, 130, 134–35

Icely, L. B., 84

January, Don, 208
Johnson, L. R., 52
Jones, Bob, 155, 162, 186, 191

Kaesche, Max, 89
Karns, Audrey, 93–94
    See also Snead, Audrey
Kelly, Chuck, 74, 75, 76, 87, 88
Kennedy, President John F., 121
Kroll, Ted, 128, 140, 182

Leonard, Stan, 117
Leopold, King of Belgium, 128
Lewis, Jerry, 130, 131
Little, Lawson, 54, 55, 97, 118
Locke, Bobby, 119, 155, 162, 163
Long, Nelson, 224
Louis, Joe, 136

McGuffin, Piggie, 120
Manahan, Mike, 75–76
Manero, Tony, 97, 98
Mangrum, Lloyd, 97, 156
Manning, Fred, 218–19
Martin, Dean, 130
Martin, Freddy, 48–50, 51–52, 53, 54, 56, 57, 59
Marx, Harpo, 130–31

Metz, Dick, 205
Middlecoff, Cary, 81, 90, 165, 167, 206
Monday, Rod, 201–3, 207

Nelson, Byron, 15, 97, 102–3, 105, 106, 108, 146, 175, 211
Nichols, Bobby, 182
Nicklaus, Jack, 138, 181, 194, 222, 229
Nixon, President Richard, 11, 121, 123–24

O'Keefe, Dennis, 134
Okie, Jack, 123

Palmer, Arnold, 72, 83, 144–45, 229
Patton, Billy Joe, 174
Picard, Henry, 57, 61, 62–63, 89, 97
Player, Gary, 181, 222

Raphael, Fred, 198
Rees, Dai, 119
Revolta, Johnny, 67, 97
Rice, Grantland, 13
Rodriguez, Chi Chi, 182, 222
Rooney, Mickey, 129–30
Runyon, Paul, 97

Sanders, Doug, 196
Sarazen Gene, 97, 167, 222
Scott, Randolph, 130
Shute, Denny, 54, 97, 106

Snead, Audrey (wife), 107, 158, 223–25
See also Karns, Audrey
Snead, Cathie (grandchild), 196
Snead, Harry (father), 16, 17, 20, 21, 25, 92
Snead, Homer (brother), 16, 19, 20, 21, 22, 23–25, 28, 29, 31, 40, 42, 58, 194
Snead, J. C. (nephew), 21, 74, 76, 189, 203, 216–17
Snead, Janet (Jenny) (sister), 16, 21, 194
Snead, Jesse (Jess) (brother), 16–17, 19, 20, 21–22, 194
Snead, Laura (mother), 16, 17–20, 23, 27, 29, 30, 41, 43–44, 74
Snead, Lyle (brother), 16, 21, 22, 23, 42, 194
Snead, Sam, Jr. (Jackie) (son), 148, 158, 195–196
Snead, Samuel Jackson, III (grandchild), 196, 228
Snead, Terrance (son), 148
Snead, Welford (Pete) (brother), 16, 21, 146, 194
Steed, Jimmy, 190
Strange, Curtis, 216
Sweden, King of, 125

Thomson, Jimmy, 158
Thomson, Peter, 197, 199
Thomson, Viola, 158
Toski, Bob, 182
Trevino, Lee, 146, 181
Tunney, Gene, 136
Turnesa, Jim, 108–11, 128
Tutweiler, Ed, 87–88, 222

Underwood, Frank ("Stetson"),
   29

Wagner, Robert, 130
Wall, Art, 133, 182, 199
Wallop, Leo, 64–65
Waring, Fred, 133
Watson, Tom, 216

Weismuller, Johnny, 130
White, Orville, 67
Williams, Ted, 135
Windsor, Duke of, 121, 125–27,
   128
Wood, Craig, 61–63, 97, 106,
   207
Worsham, Lew, 163, 164